SPECIAL NEEDS MINISTRY *for Children*

Creating a welcoming place for families whose children have special needs

PAT VERBAL
GENERAL EDITOR

Group resources really work!

This Group resource incorporates our R.E.A.L. approach to ministry. It reinforces a growing friendship with Jesus, encourages long-term learning, and results in life transformation, because it's

Relational
Learner-to-learner interaction enhances learning and builds Christian friendships.

Experiential
What learners experience through discussion and action sticks with them up to 9 times longer than what they simply hear or read.

Applicable
The aim of Christian education is to equip learners to be both hearers and doers of God's Word.

Learner-based
Learners understand and retain more when the learning process takes into consideration how they learn best.

Special Needs Ministry for Children

Creating a welcoming place for families whose children have special needs

Visit our website: **group.com**

CREDITS
General Editor: Pat Verbal
Contributing Authors: Pat Verbal, Mary Ann McPherson, Louise Tucker Jones, Jim Pierson, Larry Shallenberger, Kenneth Lay
Editors: Jennifer Hooks, Christine Yount Jones, Joani Schultz
Cover Design: Jeff Spencer
Book Design: Jean Bruns
Production: Suzi Jensen

ISBN 978-0-7644-8470-4

10 9 8 7 6 5 4 3 2   18 17 16 15 14 13

Printed in the United States of America.

TABLE OF CONTENTS

BEFORE YOU BEGIN

A Word From Joni Eareckson Tada

Dear Friend,

When a diving accident in 1967 robbed me of the use of my hands and legs, I found myself in a hospital ward wondering if I would ever smile and be hopeful again. I had become just statistical data—another member of the population affected by disabilities. And I was dangerously close to becoming a number on the list of the depressed.

The darkness lifted when friends from my church rallied around my family, offering help, hope, and positive meaning for my life. It was the church that kept us connected to reality, opening doors of possibility and paving the way for me to re-enter the mainstream of life. The church made all the difference.

My story is not unique. This is why, more than 44 years later, I'm pleased to labor alongside a worldwide staff of skilled and gifted individuals at Joni and Friends who are committed to accelerating Christian outreach into the disability community around the globe. We're energized by Jesus' statement in Luke 14:13-14a, 23b (New International Version): "But when you give a banquet, invite the poor, the crippled, the lame, the blind, and you will be blessed. Make them come in, so that my house will be full."

Yes, we're convinced that people with disabilities will be blessed, but the key is that you, too, will be blessed. When local churches reach beyond their comfort zones and embrace children with special needs and their families, the entire fellowship is blessed in dramatic ways. Your church will realize that we're richer when we recognize our poverty; we're stronger when we see our weaknesses, and we become recipients of God's grace when we understand our desperate need of him.

The book you hold in your hands, *Special Needs Ministry for Children*, is a wonderful key to unlocking the door to those blessings. As you turn each page, you'll discover practical steps on how to invite people with disabilities and their families into the fold of Christ's fellowship. You'll also read stories that will inspire and encourage you as you embark into the exciting world of disability ministry outreach.

So thank you for stepping out in this new pathway to blessing. May your heart beat in rhythm with the Savior's as you enjoy reading *Special Needs Ministry for Children*, and may God grant success as you put into practice all that you glean. After all, a ministry to children with special needs and their families involves not only a change for the family, it means a change in your church and your community. Most of all, it's about a change in you—for as you shine God's light and shake his salt, as you open up new doors of access in your church, as you reach out, one thing is sure: You will be blessed.

Joni

Joni Eareckson Tada is the founder of Joni and Friends International Disability Center, a nonprofit ministry with a global outreach. Joni's wisdom and influence have been shared with the world through bestselling books, radio programs, television programs, and frequent speaking. Her radio program is carried by 1,000 broadcast outlets and heard by over a million listeners. Joni is also an accomplished artist and singer. She has served on the National Council on Disability and the Disability Advisory Committee to the U.S. State Department. To learn more, visit Joni's Corner at www.joniandfriends.org/jonis-corner.

1

WHY YOUR CHURCH NEEDS A SPECIAL NEEDS MINISTRY

by Pat Verbal

These days it seems people expect their church to provide a staggering array of specialized ministries.

People want specific ministries for women. For men. For singles. For young marrieds. For people who've been divorced. For families. For children. For the elderly. Sometimes pastors and other church staff wonder if there's any group of three or more people that *hasn't* convinced a local church to develop a program to meet its needs.

Well, yes, there is such a group.

I belong to it.

Let me share my story...

The longest flight

As a Christian education consultant and speaker, I've spent a lot of time on airplanes. But no flight ever felt as long as the one I took a few years ago from San Francisco to Dallas.

I'd visited a mission-style bungalow in a crowded San Francisco suburb, then rushed to the airport—in tears.

As I sat on the airplane, I silently praised God for answering my prayer: I'd been able to make the trip to visit our precious 12-year-old Jessica, who has Down syndrome. Yet, here I was flying home alone. Jessica had to remain in the group home where she'd been placed for reasons beyond our control.

This sweet child who'd brought so much joy into our home was alone, growing up without her family. Growing up in a world she'd never understand.

Fighting back tears I prayed, *Lord, why can't I bring her home with me?*

When Jessica was 2 years old, she'd become part of my extended family. She instantly stole our hearts and spent many happy days in our home.

Jessica had always been small for her age, behind the norm in every area of her development. Still, she could rouse a roomful of adults up onto their feet for a chorus of "Ring Around the Rosie," and the song never ended until everyone fell down. And bedtime was always interesting because Jessica never quite understood that once you were tucked in, you were supposed to stay in bed. She got giddy when she was tired. Many nights she laughed herself to sleep.

Fighting back the tears I prayed, Lord, why can't I bring her home with me?

I missed those bedtimes. I ached for them.

At first Jessica's mother had been determined to raise Jessica in a loving, Christian home. She tried hard—very hard—but the task was too overwhelming. She struggled with exhaustion, mood swings, and depression. Eventually she seemed to give up on her marriage, her faith, and her daughter. That's when she placed Jessica in the group home.

As I flew back to Texas that fall afternoon, I tried to tell myself that Jessica was fine. The group home was clean and orderly. The housemother liked Jessica and wanted her to be happy. Jessica had proudly sung her ABCs for me, then showed me Opra, a rag doll I'd given her, perched on Jessica's bedroom pillow. Opra had been a faithful friend to Jessica, more faithful than some of the adults in her life.

Lord, why can't I bring her home with me?

So there I was, wounded, flying home to a house that no longer held my precious little one.

In San Francisco, Jessica needed the church to wrap its arms around her, welcome her, and hold her close. And headed to Texas was a weeping woman—me—who needed the same thing.

Would Jessica be welcomed and understood in your church?
Would Jessica's mother?

The need for special needs ministries

According to the World Health Organization (WHO) and the World Bank, there are 1 billion people affected by disabilities in the world.[1] If the 54 million Americans with disabilities were combined, they would roughly equal the population of California and Florida.[2] That means one in five of our fellow citizens struggles with some kind of disability. One in five! And a significant number of those are children like Jessica.

I'd love to tell you that many churches are doing a wonderful job welcoming these children, but I can't. Too many parents have disappointing stories to share…

- Belinda called several local churches when her daughter, Ellen, turned 2 years old. Cognitive and seizure disorders had kept Ellen at home since birth, and Belinda felt it was important for Ellen to have social contact with other children.

  Belinda was shocked to discover that two churches wouldn't allow Ellen to be in Sunday school at all. A third church accepted Ellen but put her in the baby nursery. When Belinda picked up Ellen, she discovered that the volunteer had left her daughter sitting in a swing the entire time.

- Kevin's experience with his son, Sammy, didn't turn out even that well.

  Sammy, an active 7-year-old, had mild autism. About half the time Sammy was in Sunday school, Kevin and his wife were called out of church to pick up Sammy. The teachers simply couldn't handle Sammy's behavior.

  Most Sundays Kevin and his wife felt like staying home and watching the service on television.

- And imagine Pam's response when she was told her 3-year-old son, Jacob, was "a little spoiled." Jacob had many sensory issues, including a strong gag reflex. This caused him to vomit frequently, especially when crying or coughing. The teacher suggested that Jacob may have vomited on purpose, just to get the class's attention.

Families affected by disabilities too often find that churches don't understand how to welcome and value their children. There simply isn't a place for them when their siblings scamper off to Sunday school classes on Sunday morning. Sadly, these children aren't the only ones who suffer.

According to Dr. Jim Pierson, president emeritus of the Christian Church Foundation for the Handicapped, families who have children with disabilities can quickly find themselves in crisis.

Many devoted parents diligently educate themselves about their children's special needs, but far too often a stressed-out mom or dad ends up leaving the family unit. The emotional and medical costs of caring for these children can severely impact families and create tremendous pressure. Siblings may also find it difficult to adjust to constantly fluctuating schedules.

The challenges of raising children with special needs are overwhelming, and many families face difficult issues without the church's involvement or support. Help for these families can be as simple as intentionally inviting their children to be part of a children's class. That alone can be a huge blessing. This book will provide practical steps to help you accomplish that task. It will also introduce you to Christian education leaders who have made the journey.

And along the way you'll be challenged to consider what you might do *beyond* Sunday morning. What can you do to provide a listening, understanding ear to a mother whose life revolves around the treatment and care of a child with special needs? How can you help the sister of that child deal with her parents' preoccupation? How can you surround that family with the love of Jesus?

Maybe you're thinking that other churches in your community are already caring for special needs children and their families, and there's no need for you to get involved.

Unfortunately, you'd likely be wrong.

Are churches serving special needs children and their families?

There are no statistics on how many churches are actively, intentionally reaching out to children with special needs and their families. But taking a look around your own neighborhood will give you a good indication. I did.

In the Dallas metropolitan area where I used to live, there are no shortages of churches. In the Greater Dallas Bell Yellow Pages, I found 15 pages of churches listed. By my figures, that came to approximately 2,600 churches. The creative ads for churches listed many ministries—worship services, choirs, hand bell choirs, Bible studies, retreats, children's programs, youth ministries, sports and recreation ministries, recovery ministries, and even a cappuccino ministry.

But not one ad highlighted a special needs ministry.

I knew of several excellent churches with disability ministries, but newcomers to Dallas apparently had to find those churches through word of mouth. By contrast, the Yellow Pages listed 11 schools for children with special needs, 19 service organizations, and page after page of medical centers specializing in a wide variety of disabilities.

Visit the websites of churches in your area. What do you see? Is there any indication that church families in your town are prepared for children with special needs? When you think of churches in your area and your own church, how do you rank the body of Christ as a source of care and hope for these families?

I believe there's room for improvement. Lots of room. This book will describe how your church can launch—or grow—a special needs ministry to children and their families.

But before we dive into the practical how-to's, let's dispel several myths…

"Our church doesn't need a special needs ministry because there aren't any children with special needs in our area."

Don't think so? Visit your local school district's website where you will find statistics on the number of students receiving some type of special education. According to the National Center for Education Statistics, these students represented about 13 percent of children and teens in 2010.[3] Or do a brief

Internet search of facilities in your town providing services to children with disabilities such as physical, occupational, and speech therapists.

Here's the truth: The children and families affected by disabilities are out there. Many of them are not in church because most churches have little to offer. If your church does offer an intentional special needs ministry, you may need to be more strategic in letting people know about your services.

"To support a special needs ministry, we need to be a big church."

The size of your church isn't important. It's the size of the congregation's heart that counts. If you believe that the Great Commission in Matthew 28 applies to everyone—including children who use wheelchairs, children who learn differently, and children who are non-verbal—then what is holding your church back? What will it take for your church to welcome and include families who need the fellowship of your congregation?

"Kids with special needs would never fit into our programming."

Sure they will! If your goal is to bring children into existing classes and programs, there are ways to adapt your activities without changing them radically.

I once visited a church with a weekly children's music program. Several children with Down syndrome in that church loved to sing. The choir director wisely selected lively songs with hand motions that allowed these children to participate in making a joyful noise to the Lord.

Another church offered a ministry that taught children how to swim in their community pool. Swimming is not an ideal fit for every child with a disability, but it can work for many children. Whatever your program, there's probably a way to accommodate children who have special needs. See Chapter 2 for some recommendations about how to make the adjustments.

"We'll have to spend a fortune fixing our building."

Not so. If your building was designed and built after 1990 in the United States, it was probably designed in compliance with the Americans with Disabilities Act (ADA), which requires that buildings be handicap accessible. That means doorways are wide enough to accommodate wheelchairs, and many barriers that interfered with the mobility of people with disabilities have been removed. More information on the ADA is discussed in Chapter 11.

But even if you meet in an older facility, it's doubtful you'll have to do much to accommodate children with disabilities and their families. You're not legally required to install elevators or retrofit bathrooms; religious organizations are exempt from the ADA's Title III requirements for public accommodations—so long as you use the building only for worship.

If any other event takes place in the building—such as a community group meeting, day care, or hosting concerts or luncheons—the ADA standards apply. If you have any questions about your facility, call the ADA Information Line at 800-514-0301 and check.

It's possible that your church building may not be held to the same standards a government building or bank has to meet. But—and here's a question for you to ponder—why would churches want to do any less?

The point of the ADA was to remove barriers that kept people from participating fully in community life. As Christians, we're all about involving people in our community of faith. Some of that happens inside the buildings where we meet. Let's not keep people out if building a wheelchair ramp will allow them in.

"Kids with special needs can get their needs met elsewhere. That's what group homes are for."

We thank God for well-run group homes, as well as for caring professionals who meet children's physical and emotional needs. Many of them do a tremendous job.

But a group home isn't a church. Teaching children about God isn't part of the daily routine or even part of most group homes' mission statements.

Expecting group homes to encourage children to know, love, and follow Jesus would be like expecting hospitals where kids go for surgery to provide treatments for their spiritual health. Doctors don't specialize in that; they're focused on correcting a birth defect or removing a life-threatening blockage.

The church can't delegate its responsibility for nurturing the faith of children to outside agencies. Rather, we need to partner with parents to help them assume their God-given role as primary faith shapers. It's the church's job to pray for the works of God in the hearts of our children.

"We don't have anyone here who can handle children with unique needs."

It's true that working with children who are "different" requires some training. But working in a special needs ministry doesn't require a degree in special education or a teaching credential. In this book you'll read about churches that launched effective ministries with little or no experience beyond a desire to serve children and a heart for God. There's ample opportunity for training from community agencies, parents of kids with disabilities, and mentoring from professionals.

Don't let the lack of training slow you down. Chapter 7 suggests ways you can quickly get your staff and volunteers up to speed. If you're a typical church, there's nothing stopping you from reaching out to children and families affected by disabilities.

Nothing but a decision holds you back from starting a special needs ministry.

What exactly is a "special needs ministry"?

A special needs ministry is simply an intentional ministry aimed at meeting the physical, intellectual, and emotional needs of children with disabilities.

The Golden Hills Community Church in Brentwood, California, summed it up well in their special needs mission statement. Their goals are: "To make disciples within the disabled community by demonstrating Christ's love and equipping the congregation to minister to their special needs so that all might fellowship, worship, and serve."

Special needs are disabilities that prevent children from progressing at the typical pace of their peers. Some are visible—others are not. The various kinds of disabilities are extremely diverse, but categories share common characteristics. If you create a special needs ministry, you can count on at least some of your kids demonstrating…

- hyperactivity with short attention spans
- distractibility and impulsiveness
- poor visual/motor skills and poor large-muscle and fine-motor coordination

- rapid and excessive changes of mood and reasoning
- faulty perception with repetition of a thought or action
- problems with social interaction and inconsistent and unpredictable behavior

Will these be the "easiest" children to manage in class? Some will, but many will not...but they may well be the most willing to learn. The most willing to serve. The most willing to share God's love with family and friends.

And they may well make a significant difference in your church and the world as they live out their faith.

Mark Thompson is a gifted musical ventriloquist who says he was an ADD (attention-deficit disorder) child. "I'm often asked how I carry on a lively conversation with a puppet on each hand," says Mark. "I tell people that's just the way my mind works. I function best when I'm focused and going full speed ahead."

As a child, Mark was hyperactive, loud, and describes himself as "often annoying." He wanted to learn, but found it hard to control himself and to stop talking. In spite of his behavior, his teachers at church managed to make him feel loved and accepted.

"My father also had problems in school because he couldn't read well," says Mark. "People called him a dummy. So instead of finishing high school, he worked in a garden." The only book that Mark ever saw his father pick up was the Bible.

As a child, Mark was hyperactive, loud, and describes himself as "often annoying."

Mark is thankful for mentors who gave him love and guidance. He prays for children with ADD to know God. "I entertain thousands of people each year and train church teachers to plug these kids in with responsibility, structure, and ownership. They can shine for Jesus." To learn about Mark's ministry visit his website at markthompson.org.

A special needs ministry would welcome children like Mark and value them. And it would provide a shoulder on which weary parents could lean for support.

What will a special needs ministry do for your church?

For starters, you'll be fulfilling the Great Commission.

Nowhere in Jesus' command that the gospel be shared with the world does he add a qualifier that only the able-bodied need be contacted. If anything, Jesus showed a special compassion for those who were ill, blind, or lame—ones who might be candidates for a special needs ministry.

While visiting a church in Alabama, I was escorted by the pastor to a front-row seat. That's when I noticed the young people filling the pew next to me. Many of them had Down syndrome. Others were in wheelchairs. I returned their smiles and waves as the organist began to play.

The young people were obviously delighted with their special spot. During the worship music, a girl picked up her papers and moved to a different seat—just because. A boy held his song book upside down and sang off key, but with gusto. Another rushed down the aisle, talked to a gentleman, and scurried back to his place. During greeting time, I was bombarded by handshakes and hugs. I couldn't understand their words, but their enthusiasm brought tears to my eyes.

I couldn't help but notice how loving the pastors were to their "front-row crowd." Many in the congregation also took extra care to greet them and engage in conversation.

This was so different from what I'd seen in churches that I asked the pastor about it. "If Jesus were here today," he said, "we believe he would be leading a special needs ministry. He had such a heart for those who seemed to get left out."

Who wouldn't want their church to be a place like that—where nobody gets left out?

You'll reflect God's love in your community.

A common criticism of today's Church is that it simply isn't relevant. There is plenty of preaching but it has no pulse, no connection to real life. This is certainly not the case when your church is meeting real, felt needs like those of children and their families coping with disabilities.

Nella Uitvlugt, Director of Friendship Ministries in Michigan, helps churches start well-rounded special needs programs. Part of what she does is persuade churches to consider their ministries as resources for families as a whole. Noting that an adult who was raised with a sibling with a disability can carry crippling baggage into adulthood, Uitvlugt says, "Let's deal with these family issues while children are young. Some siblings may have to do more babysitting than other kids. They may not be able to participate in outside activities because there just isn't time, energy, and money to go around."

Your special needs ministry can be more than simply a ministry to a child—though that would be reason enough to support a ministry. You can also support parents, siblings, and extended family members who love and serve the child with special needs.

You'll invite some truly amazing people into your midst.

During praise and worship one Sunday, out of the corner of my eye I saw Helen heading straight toward me. Clutching a piece of typing paper tightly in her fist, she wrapped her arms around my neck, gave me a quick hug, pushed the paper into my hand, and bounced back to her seat.

Looking down I saw green, red, blue, and yellow hearts drawn with a shaky hand. The large, out-of-proportion print read, "To Pat from Helen for Valentines. I love you."

Helen is a petite young woman who was a blessing our church. Her speech was difficult to understand, but she clearly embodied the childlike faith Jesus described in Luke 18:16b-17: "Then Jesus called for the children and said to the disciples, 'Let the children come to me. Don't stop them! For the Kingdom of God belongs to those who are like these children. I tell you the truth, anyone who doesn't receive the Kingdom of God like a child will never enter it.' "

You'll grow a generation of children who are tolerant and accepting of people with special needs.

As children interact with their peers who have special needs, walls come down...fears subside...and curiosity is replaced with compassion. Make it a goal of your children's ministry to teach kids without disabilities that God doesn't make mistakes. Show them that the kingdom of God includes all people, especially people who are different from them. Everyone who loves and serves Jesus is a brother or sister in God's family.

You'll assimilate families into your church.

If you start a special needs ministry, it's highly unlikely you'll suddenly double the size of your congregation. Special needs ministries may not attract large groups of people—but they will draw families who will truly appreciate your church's focus and heart for ministry.

Families who live with the demands of a disability have great lessons to teach us. God's power and grace are visible in these families, and as we share their struggles we rely more on God in our own lives. Churches that reach out to these families are also promised a blessing in return. "Instead, invite the poor, the crippled, the lame, and the blind. Then at the resurrection of the righteous, God will reward you for inviting those who could not repay you" (Luke 14:13-14).

BACKED IN THE WORD

Is there theological support for developing a special needs ministry in your church?

Yes—without a doubt! The following summary is from a document on disabilities by the National Council of Churches (ncccusa.org). It clearly outlines a biblical foundation for serving all people.

1. God created all people in his image (Genesis 1:26). This image is not a measurable set of characteristics. God's image is reflected uniquely in each person.

2. God calls all people (Matthew 11:28). Disabilities in no way preclude someone from being valued by God.

Seek understanding first

In many ways, a special needs ministry is much like any effective ministry. It must include an understanding of the people we wish to serve—children with special needs, of course, but also their families.

Mary Ann McPherson can help us better appreciate what life is like when you live in a world of special needs around the clock. She's a Christian educator and also the mother of a young lady with Down syndrome. In the next chapter, Mary Ann will describe the life she and her family lead. Then you'll dive into the nuts and bolts of what it takes to establish or expand a church-based special needs ministry.

But first, take a few moments to reflect on your ministry. Throughout this book you'll find "Just for you" sections. Don't skip past these brief passages. Think of them as quick opportunities to pause, be refreshed, and to let God speak to you about the ministry role he may be unfolding for you.

3. All people have special gifts (1 Corinthians 12:4). All people collectively need the gifts God has given each person, and no one is unnecessary.

4. God invites all people to participate in his ministry (1 Corinthians 12:7). God continually empowers each member of the body of Christ to serve and benefit the church and the broader community.

5. Jesus called children to himself—without exceptions (Matthew 19:14). There's nothing Jesus ever said or did during his time on Earth to suggest that children who are on crutches or in wheelchairs, intellectually disabled, or victims of abuse should not come to him. Can we do less?

Just for you

We often see images of Jesus hanging on the cross. He's usually pictured bloodied and battered, grimacing in pain. Yet he looks down with a compassion that shines straight from his breaking heart.

Think about that scene from a different perspective for a moment. Think about who's standing beneath the cross, scattered across the hillside, looking up.

A mother watching her son die, one breath at a time, yet unable to help him.

A shattered man who has betrayed his closest friend.

A Roman soldier just now beginning to sense that an innocent man hangs silhouetted against the darkening sky, nailed to fierce, blood-stained wood.

Perhaps a man who once was hopelessly crippled, but who now could walk the crooked path up to the Place of the Skull.

There was room for all these people at the foot of the cross. There's room there for everyone. It doesn't matter if a person arrives on foot or in a wheelchair. Whether the person stands sightless, unable to hear, or unable to speak.

There's room for us all.

Thanks for reaching across the obstacles that special needs can create to share this message: There's room for you.

Dear God,

You love us all. Thank you for the chance to reach out with the good news of your gospel to children with special needs and their families. There is room for everyone at the foot of the cross. And there's room for us all in your church.

In Jesus' name, amen.

ENDNOTES

1 World Health Organization (WHO) http://tinyurl.com/3av9ebg

2 U.S. Census Bureau, http://www.census.gov/newsroom/releases/archives/income_wealth/cb08-185.html

3 http://nces.ed.gov/programs/coe/indicator_cwd.asp

2

WHAT DO FAMILIES WITH SPECIAL NEEDS CHILDREN NEED?

by Mary Ann McPherson

Sarah is the youngest of our three daughters. She has silky blonde hair. Big blue eyes. A charming, ear-to-ear smile.

And Sarah has Down syndrome.

From the moment a neonatal specialist told us there might be a genetic problem with Sarah, I sensed that every person in my life—family, friends, neighbors, and even acquaintances—were being drawn together in a circle around our family.

When our first two daughters were born, it was a circle of celebration.

This time it was a circle of concern.

And in a way we'd never experienced before, my husband and I became vulnerable and needy.

We needed to grieve

When a family discovers their child has a disability, it's often a time of crisis. There's no timetable for how long it takes to work through the news, but many family members go through the predictable stages of grief: denial, bargaining, anger, depression, and eventual acceptance.

Parents and other close family members mourn the child they imagined would be born. A young mother once told me, "The moment the doctors said, 'It's a girl,' my thoughts raced with visions of ballet lessons, proms, academic scholarships, and a wedding dress. Then I heard the words *Down syndrome*, and all those dreams were shattered."

For many parents, like this mom, there's a time when their child's disability overshadows the very essence of the person God created in their child. For some, grief becomes part of their life for years. Birthdays become a reminder of a child's lagging development. Upon meeting a typically developing child who's the same age, parents can't help but make unwelcome comparisons. Another painful reminder can be to watch a younger sibling developing beyond their older child who has special needs.

The first few months following a diagnosis of "disability" can be an emotionally fragile time for parents. These parents need helpful friends who'll be examples of Proverbs 18:24b: "A real friend sticks closer than a brother."

My husband Dave and I had some of those friends in our lives. They cooked for us, hugged us, and told us that they loved us. They acted as a buffer by passing on information. They gave us permission to cry and watched our other daughters when Sarah had medical appointments.

They listened and treated Sarah like any other newborn.

And most importantly, they prayed for us daily as we grieved.

We needed to survive the emotional roller coaster

One thing you can assume is true for any parent whose young child has a disability: mom or dad is emotionally drained.

The parents of an infant facing open-heart surgery shared, "We bounced from feeling peaceful and accepting of the place God had us into a total panic about the future, feeling that God had abandoned us. There were days we couldn't see past the day of surgery, and then there were days we worried about what life would be like for all of us in 40 years."

Parents' emotions can often be filtered through the way they perceive a specific disability. That means what they know—or think they know—can have a huge impact on how they feel.

Other factors that impact a parent's response include their personal experiences with persons with disabilities. Have those experiences been positive or negative? Also, how well-grounded is the parent spiritually? What sort of support is the parent receiving from friends and family? Life may become emotionally complicated when parents feel the need to comfort others or defend their beliefs about their child's disorder.

It was difficult for me to face our neighbors and church family the first few months after Sarah was born. I felt so unsteady at any given moment.

I also quickly discovered that some people were so uncomfortable with Sarah that they avoided our family. Others poured out their sympathy. Still others were encouraging.

I know there are parents of children with special needs who take a deep breath when they hear a diagnosis and then move on without hesitation. But that wasn't me. I needed to grieve deeply, and my husband and dearest friends gave me the time and support to do so. Through my tears and prayers, I found that God was closer than he had ever been in my life. I knew for certain I was not alone and that God would give me wisdom and strength whenever I called on him.

Parents whose child has been diagnosed with a disability sometimes go through long periods of denial. They believe their child is only mildly affected and with a little therapy will be fine.

But then if their son or daughter fails to develop as they had hoped, these parents sink into deep grief. They come to understand their hopes won't be rewarded, that their assumptions were incorrect.

What they asked God to do isn't going to happen.

I wrote this entry in my journal when Sarah was 12 days old:

Diane, our neighbor who's also a member of our church, came over late this afternoon with a baby gift. She oohed and aahed over Sarah and asked enthusiastically to hold her. I nervously explained the details of Sarah's birth and at the end I blurted out, "She has Down syndrome."

"I've heard that," replied Diane. This news was no big deal for her. She treated my baby as she would any other baby. I felt so encouraged. She gave me a copy of "Welcome to Holland."

Then came the tears. I cried because I want so desperately to see the joys that Sarah will bring. And I cried because I still don't want to be here.

Grief takes whatever time it takes. Are you allowing families whose children are disabled to take the time they need to grieve?

We needed to face the unknown—and our fear

Parents of a child with a disability are quickly ushered into a foreign world.

It's the world of hospitals and medical specialists. A world that may include cardiologists, orthopedic specialists, genetic specialists, neurologists, physical therapists, occupational therapists, and early intervention specialists. A world crowded with medical appointments and frustrating insurance forms no one can understand, no one can fill out perfectly.

And a world in which there's no way parents can know how their child's disability will impact the future—their child's future and their family's future.

We all feel concern about how our children will fare in the future. Imagine how you'd feel if you knew with certainty that your child required constant attention and care to survive—and that the day might come when you weren't there to provide it. The future becomes a dark and scary place.

Parents in your church who have children with disabilities need to be reminded they can cling to God because he's faithful, never-changing, and omnipotent. Deuteronomy 7:9 says, "Understand, therefore, that the Lord your God is indeed God. He is the faithful God who keeps his covenant for a thousand generations and lavishes his unfailing love on those who love him and obey his commands."

God is in charge of the future.

Parents aren't.

How are you helping families face the unknown with faith and confidence? And what help can you provide for interacting with the agencies, medical facilities, and turmoil that comes with shuttling a child from appointment to appointment?

We needed to have our child build relationships with typically developing children

Many children with disabilities have few friends with whom they play outside of a school setting. This is sad not only for these children but for their typical peers as well.

Children with special needs benefit from relationships because the contact helps build their social skills. They'll try harder to do the same tasks as their typical friends and be better prepared to live in the community.

All children benefit from exposure to the disability community by becoming more sensitive, patient, positive, and tolerant. They'll gain a more accurate view of individual differences. They can also enjoy positive experiences with individuals who model success despite their challenges.

Entering and sustaining play is one of the more difficult social accomplishments that typically developing children learn during their early years. A child with a disability will most likely need to learn to do this first by having a competent adult play partner. Having an adult close by will help the child know what to say and do when interacting with their peers.

And that can't happen for Sarah without there being some typically developing children around willing to play and interact.

Here's a glimpse of what it's like

A group of parents whose children were diagnosed on the autism spectrum made a list of their top-10 needs and concerns. They shared the list with me at a workshop:

- Sleep (and the rest that comes with it)
- Coping with family members' reactions
- Coping with friends' reactions
- Understanding what they did wrong to have disabled children
- Wondering if they've done enough to help their children
- Worrying about siblings not getting enough time or attention

- Dealing with the effects on their marriage
- Worrying about their children's future: Will their children have jobs?
- Worrying about their children's future: Will their children be safe?
- Worrying about their children's future: Who will love their children when the parents die?

Any parent can relate to some of the items on the list. Most parents have war stories about sleepless nights, embarrassing tantrums at the grocery store, sibling battles, and trips to the emergency room.

> Who will love their children when the parents die?

But parents of children with disabilities will probably experience those trials with greater intensity, and the trials will last longer. It's not uncommon for these children to experience insomnia on a regular basis or need medical intervention for months or even years at a time.

My friend's little girl has slept through the night just three times in four years. Another mother has two children with a food absorption disorder. Keeping them alive and healthy required her to give them medication through stomach feeding tubes every four hours, around the clock, throughout their infancy and early childhood years.

Look again at the list. Ask parents coping with disabilities if it strikes a chord and if they'd add something to the list.

You can't minister effectively to families until you understand their lives; the daily realities that these parents are living, day after day, week after week, and perhaps forever.

Do you understand? Can you begin to adapt your church's programming to be in sync with their daily lives? If you can, it will be like ministry to Jesus himself. He told us of this when he said, "And the King will say, 'I tell you the truth, when you did it to one of the least of these my brothers and sisters, you were doing it to me!' " (Matthew 25:40 NLT).

Here's a glimpse of what it's like to be in a family that has a child with special needs...

The demands are relentless.

When you're raising a son or daughter with special needs, developmental timetables are irrelevant. It's common for your child to experience developmental delays in one or more areas. He may lag behind his peers physically, verbally, emotionally, and academically. This means that, even though the child experiences growth in the same predictable sequence as classmates without disabilities, your child's development seems to occur in slow motion.

Disabled children are typically more dependent on their parents for a longer period of time. Self-help skills such as dressing, bathing, and toileting may be significantly delayed.

Imagine for a moment doubling or tripling the amount of time spent in every stage that your typically developing child has gone through. Instead of changing diapers for two to three years, you buy and change diapers for four to six years. Instead of carrying your baby up and down stairs for 10 to 13 months, you carry your child for two to three years. This kind of constant caregiving can be physically and emotionally draining on parents, siblings, and extended family members.

Imagine doubling or tripling the time spent in every stage your typically developing child has gone through.

It's challenging for siblings.

Having a child with unique medical or developmental needs often means that balancing time and attention for other kids in the family is extremely difficult.

"It's just not fair" isn't simply a whiny complaint when applied to siblings in a family coping with complicated disabilities. It's an accurate statement.

The daily requirements of a child with special needs can easily overshadow the needs of typically developing brothers and sisters. It's normal for the child who's most dependent to receive the lion's share of time and consideration from parents...but it certainly isn't fair.

Scheduling extracurricular activities for the nondisabled children in a family can be a nightmare when added to the appointments and money spent taking brother or sister to physical, speech, or occupational therapy, doctor's visits, and other related commitments. And if the sibling with disabilities has related behavior problems, even the most empathetic sibling can feel angry, embarrassed, or discouraged when a child has an unpredictable meltdown in public.

Remember that the child with the disability isn't always the baby in the family. An older child with a disability who's aware of his or her limitations may also be sad or resentful of the situation. And younger siblings may be embarrassed by the limitations of their older brother or sister.

Parents are stressed to the max.

Couples who have children with disabilities are at tremendous risk for separation and divorce.

There are money issues: The medical needs and ongoing therapy may quickly overwhelm the family budget.

Sometimes only one parent—usually the mother—is in charge of arranging and transporting the child to a multitude of appointments. That can lead to feelings of resentment and isolation in both parents. The problem can be further exacerbated if there's no extended family or friends to help with caregiving. Couples may have to rely on each other for a break, and that tag-team approach leaves little or no time alone to nurture their relationship. It can become an exhausting way to live.

Not every parent of a child with a disability is constantly challenged to find ways of avoiding problem situations. Some children's disabilities are milder, causing less turmoil and stress. Family members are eventually able to fall into daily routines that seem almost effortless. But never doubt it—these families also long for acceptance, friendship, and a loving church family.

If there are families affected by disability in your church, you can walk alongside them by providing very practical ministry that starts with listening. Friends who ask us how our life is going and how they can pray for us help us to feel we're not alone.

One couple, whose children were in Sarah's Sunday school class, even learned a few words in sign language when they heard Sarah was learning to communicate that way. It's a great feeling to have someone love your child who's not a paid professional.

It's a great feeling to have someone love your child who's not a paid professional.

Babysitters are lifesavers.

It's not easy for parents of typical children to find babysitters. It's almost impossible for parents of children with special needs to find babysitters who can communicate with nonverbal children, feed children who are unable to feed themselves, or manage the behavior of an unpredictable child.

Parents of children with special needs are still couples—and need time to invest in their marriage relationship. They need date nights. They need time away. Capable babysitters are of immeasurable value. Even offering to watch the other siblings while mom or dad takes a child to therapy can be a welcome relief.

Networking becomes essential.

There are times when it's helpful for parents of children with disabilities to talk to one another. Parents can share their experiences, feel understood, and develop a network of resources. Networks also provide a broader base of ideas for handling whatever situation families are facing.

Is your church providing networking opportunities for parents? If not, here's what families affected by disabilities need.

Here's what families affected by disabilities need

We need unconditional love and acceptance.

God calls us to love each other in a way that's unconditional—and rare. While I wish I could expect Sarah to receive unconditional love in the world, I can't. But I can anticipate that she'll encounter it at church.

Why am I so sure? Because Sarah gives others her unconditional love at church. She touches people's lives with her smile and acceptance. I see it in the eyes and hugs of her Sunday school teachers as they welcome her into children's worship. I see it when other parents greet her in the hallway between services. She reaches out—and friends reach back. Those who look beyond Sarah's disability see the young lady that God created.

Not every child is able to reach out, to express love. Maybe you feel uncomfortable around kids who are different. You're not sure of what to do or say.

Here's what to do: Decide to walk in Jesus' steps. Decide to love—unconditionally.

The Bible says, "For I can do everything through Christ, who gives me strength" (Philippians 4:13). But do we believe it? We often quote Romans 8:28,

"And we know that God causes everything to work together for the good of those who love God and are called according to his purpose for them." But do we act like it?

Do we look at children with special needs through the eyes of God's love? That's what my family needs. That's what every family needs.

We need caring and informed Sunday school teachers.

Of course, I haven't always looked at children with disabilities the way I do now. I was trained to be an early childhood development specialist, an expert in typical child development.

I didn't want to teach "those" children. I didn't have a clue how to teach them. I felt uncomfortable around children with special needs. What would I say? What if I couldn't understand them? What if they didn't respond to me?

Parents of typically developing children usually find great programs for their kids at church. These parents can refuel with worship and teaching as their children learn with peers elsewhere in the building.

WRITE SOCIAL STORIES ABOUT CHURCH

You can use visual or written social stories as a tool for teaching social skills to children with autism and related disabilities. Social stories give children facts about new situations that they may find confusing. Describe the church and classroom focusing on a few key points: the expected reactions of greeters or teachers, actions that might be expected of a child, and why. The goal of the story is to increase the child's understanding and to make him or her more comfortable with a new experience.

Not so for all parents who bring their children to church. Parents of children with unique needs often feel vulnerable for themselves and for their child. It's difficult to encounter people who don't understand and who aren't always welcoming.

Plus, most families find that going to church is a nice break from their daily routines. But that's a problem for children who thrive on routine, which is a vital learning tool. Taking these kids somewhere new or changing their Sunday school teachers can have devastating effects.

An unfamiliar routine, such as visiting a new church, can be extremely stressful. Parents may not be able to predict how their child will react or how church members will react to their child. Something as simple as a poster with pictures and labels explaining the Sunday school hour can make a huge difference in the behavior of a child with special needs.

This special needs family feels understood at church

I met Bill and Karen Freeman and their 5-year-old daughter, Rebecca, through a Mothers of Preschoolers (MOPS) group. Rebecca was born with Down syndrome. Some years later, I asked Bill and Karen when, in their experience with churches, they've felt truly understood.

Here's what I heard…

"We felt understood when we felt refreshed."

To maintain a positive attitude during the ongoing challenge of caring for their child, Bill and Karen needed fellowship and Bible study. When a teacher took charge of Rebecca's special needs so they could go to Sunday school together, they felt refreshed and their faith grew.

Another refreshing moment came when a friend supervised Rebecca for 10 minutes so Bill and Karen could enjoy a short, meaningful conversation with a friend in the church's welcome center.

Are the parents of children with special needs in your church experiencing spiritual refreshment? What can you do to help?

"We felt understood when we didn't have to do it all ourselves."

Bill and Karen did what many parents who have children with disabilities do: They took responsibility for activities that included their daughter. But after serving as Rebecca's Sunday school teacher, children's music leader, and Girl Scout leader, they discovered they were isolated from outlets and activities they needed as adults.

In addition, they were tired.

That's when Bill and Karen let go of the expectation they had to do it all. And they were relieved when other capable adults stepped in to fill those roles.

Is it your expectation that if a child with special needs is involved in your program, the parent needs to be involved as well? Do the parents in your ministry believe that's the case?

WELCOME TO HOLLAND

by Emily Perl Kingsley

I am often asked to describe the experience of raising a child with a disability—to try to help people who have not shared that unique experience to understand it, to imagine how it would feel. It's like this...

When you're going to have a baby, it's like planning a fabulous vacation trip—to Italy. You buy a bunch of guidebooks and make your wonderful plans. The Coliseum. The Michelangelo David. The gondolas in Venice. You may learn some handy phrases in Italian. It's all very exciting.

After months of eager anticipation, the day finally arrives. You pack your bags and off you go. Several hours later, the plane lands. The stewardess comes in and says, "Welcome to Holland."

"Holland?" you say. "What do you mean Holland? I signed up for Italy! I'm supposed to be in Italy. All my life I've dreamed of going to Italy."

But there's been a change in the flight plan. They've landed in Holland and there you must stay.

"We felt understood when church staff communicated with us about our daughter."

For Bill and Karen, it was a relief to know that their church staff understood Rebecca's needs, challenges, and strengths.

Each new school year presented the same challenge: What class should she be in? Who would help her? Was the social contact important enough to keep her with children her age? Was this the best place for her to learn what is important for her spiritual growth?

Bill and Karen coached Rebecca's teachers and helpers until they felt comfortable leaving her in class. But unfortunately, this communication sometimes faltered when church volunteers frequently changed schedules each quarter.

And when one church didn't understand Rebecca or have the needed

The important thing is that they haven't taken you to a horrible, disgusting, filthy place full of pestilence, famine, and disease. It's just a different place.

So you must go out and buy new guidebooks. And you must learn a whole new language. And you will meet a whole new group of people you would never have met.

It's just a different place. It's slower paced than Italy, less flashy than Italy. But after you've been there for a while and you catch your breath, you look around...and you begin to notice that Holland has windmills...and Holland has tulips. Holland even has Rembrandts.

But everyone you know is busy coming and going from Italy...and they're all bragging about what a wonderful time they had there. And for the rest of your life, you will say, "Yes, that's where I was supposed to go. That's what I had planned."

And the pain of that will never, ever, ever, ever go away...because the loss of that dream is a very, very significant loss.

But...if you spend your life mourning the fact that you didn't get to Italy, you may never be free to enjoy the very special, the very lovely things...about Holland.

resources, Bill and Karen felt forced to moved to a church that practiced better communication and was ready to help. The cost of not making such a move would be to let Rebecca slip through the cracks. For any parent, that's an unacceptable cost.

How are you communicating with parents of children with special needs in your church?

"We felt understood when church programs made room for Rebecca."

Rebecca participated in vacation Bible school, children's chorus, summer music camp, and Sunday school. Because those programs highlighted drama and music as teaching mediums, Rebecca could participate and function well. Those are settings in which she flourished.

Rebecca was also welcomed in group activities because church leaders provided parental involvement and adaptive assistance.

Which of your children's ministry programs are truly open to children with special needs?

"We felt understood when Rebecca was able to do ministry as well as receive it."

Bill and Karen were pleased that their church understood Rebecca and included her. When she was old enough, she was allowed to serve as a teacher's helper in the Sunday preschool ministry. Their daughter was able to be a fully functioning, giving member of Christ's body.

And that glorifies God in amazing ways.

Just for you

It's easy to think of a special needs ministry for children as just that—for children. But that's not true. It also blesses parents and siblings. It can provide precious time for a married couple to enjoy a cup of coffee or attend worship together. It may give a tired mommy a chance to take other children to the mall for some uninterrupted one-on-one time.

You're reaching out to children, but your loving touch reaches others, too. What an impact you're having in families' lives!

Dear God,

Thank you that serving you is often like dropping a stone in a quiet lake—the ripples stretch out and reach far beyond our expectations. Bless the families of the children our ministry serves.

In Jesus' name, amen.

3

THE SPECIAL NEEDS MINISTRY LAUNCH COUNTDOWN CHECKLIST

by Pat Verbal

You're thinking of launching a special needs ministry or expanding the ministry already under way in your church.

Before you take that next step, here's a quick checklist of four things to do now.

☑ **Check** your church culture

Not too many years ago, the only portrayals of individuals with disabilities on television or in movies were negative ones. The world viewed them as "damaged goods" to be avoided. People who were different simply didn't fit the culture's notion of heroes, no matter how smart, courageous, or caring they were. Thankfully, things are changing in some areas and walls are coming down between the church and the disability community.

Movies such as *I Am Sam, Forrest Gump,* and *Temple Grandin* have helped viewers relate to people with disability and appreciate their strengths. In the TV series *Parenthood* viewers watched a loving family grow closer as they faced the challenges of raising a son with Asperger's syndrome. Talented personalities such as Michael J. Fox and Heather Whitestone McCallum, a former Miss America who is deaf, have become positive role models for children with and without disabilities.

The business world is also recognizing the importance of serving families affected by disability. AMC Theatres hosts movie matinees for children with autism and other developmental disorders. The theaters' lights and sounds are lower. Kids can bring in toys and special snacks. Parents can also bring siblings without worrying about their child with special needs making noise or moving around during the movie. Even Disney World is providing special equipment, advice, support, and options for children with unique needs.

If culture can change, why not the church? Look around. Are congregations in your community more welcoming to children and adults with disabilities now than they were 10 years ago?

While families affected by disability may be more visible, churches still have a long way to go. For example, do people with disabilities fill places of ministry and leadership in today's churches? Not many. Could that be because churches still see people with disabilities as those who don't fit in rather than looking at them from a biblical view?

The first step in establishing a special needs ministry is to determine what your church thinks of people with disabilities. Are they outsiders? Or are they something different?

Just asking the question won't necessarily get you an honest answer. Few people will risk being politically incorrect by saying, "Well, yes, I really don't see a place for a child with Down syndrome here."

The way to tell if your church's culture is open to people with disabilities is to evaluate what your church does, not what your leadership says. Check the fruit of your ministry.

How to Determine the Way Your Church Really Feels About People With Special Needs

The fact that your church doesn't have a special needs ministry doesn't make you an uncaring congregation. Far from it.

According to Focus on the Family founder Dr. James Dobson, the church as a whole is not meeting the needs of people with disabilities. Most churches don't have intentional programs that include the weakest among us—though there are exceptions.

In a broadcast titled "Mothers of Handicapped Children," Dr. Dobson pointed out the obvious: When people who have special needs come to church and realize there's no one like themselves there, they leave—and never come back.

Said Dr. Dobson, "I really feel that the Christian church is going to have to examine its values at this point, because there but for the grace of God go I or my child."

Like Dr. Dobson, most Christians readily agree that special needs ministry is important. They express great appreciation for people who serve in this area. So what's the problem? Why aren't there more ministries up and running?

I think the problem comes when churches try to identify their role in reaching families who don't fit into the church's traditional programs. The notion of launching new programs strikes fear in the hearts of church staff. Who will oversee them? fund them? staff them? When it's a major problem trying to get enough Sunday school teachers, how can churches even think of creating a new program?

Often a desire to start a special needs ministry dies right there on the launching pad—shot down before it's even attempted. Yet your church believes that children with special needs must be given an opportunity to hear and respond to God's good news. Nobody is voting against the notion that God calls people with special needs to him.

Do this: Determine what your church truly believes by using the following assessment tool. Take note of the description that reflects what you're doing—not what you're saying—on this Action Assessment Line. The tool is adapted from one created by Dr. Scott Daniels and Dr. Steve Green.

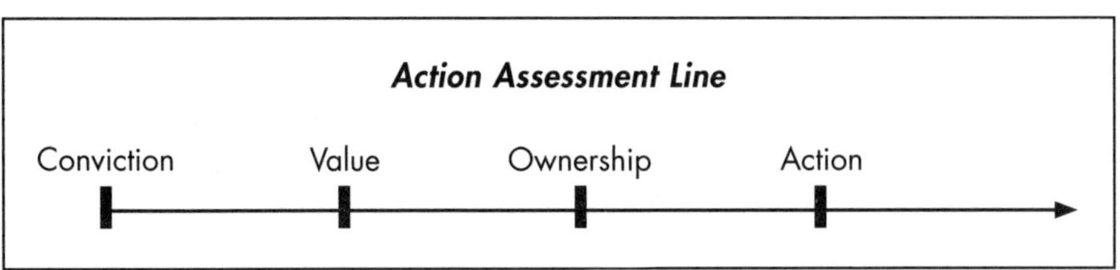

☑ ***Conviction*** is the belief that something should be done by someone but not necessarily by your church. Your church leaders are here if their responses to your questions about launching a special needs ministry sound like this one: "It's a great idea and something we should definitely put on a future agenda for discussion and exploration." This is especially true if your church already has children with special needs—but there's no programming to meet their needs.

☑ ***Value*** is the next step toward taking action. It's recognizing that the "good idea" actually connects to part of the church's mission statement, that it reflects the church's values, and that being intentional about including families who have children with special needs might fit into a vision for sharing the gospel with your community. If the response of your church leadership is along the lines of "We can see how that would help us accomplish our mission," then place a mark on "value."

☑ ***Ownership*** happens when there are people in your church who already have responsibility for this sort of ministry. Typically special needs ministries enter a church through the children's ministry, but not always. If your leadership says, "That sounds like something Nancy should be handling," then you're in the orbit of ownership.

Of course, if Nancy is an already-overworked, part-time children's pastor who has no idea where to begin with a special needs ministry, ownership may be a mirage. Until someone looks you in the eye and says, "I'll do it," or gives you permission to move ahead yourself, you don't have authentic ownership.

☑ ***Action*** occurs when you actually begin shaping your church's special needs ministry. Your church leadership has given you its blessing—or at least its permission—to start. You have a budget, though it may be humble. You have the opportunity to report back to the leadership what you're doing, why you're doing it, and what you hope to accomplish.

You know you've finally arrived at the action step when you can put news about a special needs ministry in the bulletin or on the website, and people begin to show interest.

What is your church's culture regarding special needs ministry? Where did you place a mark on the line? It's good to know where you are because that's your starting point.

Your goal is to move your church leadership and the whole congregation from the conviction end of the Action Assessment Line toward the action end. That's where things happen.

Three Tools at Your Disposal

1. Prayer

Nothing can substitute for spending time in prayer. Pray for your church pastors, staff, and leadership teams. Ask God to help you remain sensitive to his timing. Pray for the families this ministry can reach. Pray for staff and volunteers to emerge. Pray for your own motives and a godly vision of your ministry. Pray for grace, patience, and love.

2. Passion

It's been said nothing happens in the church until there's an advocate who's willing to make it happen. There's some truth in that statement, though it's also true that advocates need to quickly make friends who'll help shoulder the load. Are you that advocate? Are there people willing to help you?

The demand for caring volunteers who'll take a ministry and run with it is huge for church leaders. It's one thing for you to meet with your pastor and say, "Someone really ought to do something." It's another thing to add, "And I'm that someone."

Are you that someone?

3. Education

Chuck Colson, founder of Prison Fellowship, served seven months of a 1- to 3-year prison sentence after pleading guilty in 1974 to Watergate-related charges. Colson's ministry leads thousands of Christians to volunteer as mentors for prisoners and to care for their families, sharing the gospel of Jesus Christ. A sought-after speaker and award-winning author, he educated the Church on its 21st-century struggle between a secular and a biblical worldview before his death in 2012.

In his later years, Colson became a strong advocate on another topic—children with special needs. His eyes lit up when he talked about his relationship with his grandson, Max, who has autism.

Dr. Chuck Swindoll, a long-time supporter of disability ministries, has become a stronger voice for special needs since his grandson John was diagnosed with autism.

These leaders represent hundreds of others whose families have been impacted by a child or grandchild with special needs. These realities are educating the church on the importance of including children with special needs. These issues take on a new significance when disability hits home.

The question, though, is: Should we wait until we're personally faced with a disability to move a disability ministry up on our list of priorities? In the same way that suddenly losing the use of your hand would remind you that your hand has been faithfully serving you for a lifetime without you giving it any thought, so does having a real, live person enter your building in a wheelchair remind you that a special needs ministry is important.

Suddenly a vague belief that your church should think through how to minister to those with special needs gets big-time attention.

You can educate your church leaders in several ways. Here are some suggestions:

Provide literature and statistics. Some leaders want to know the numbers. Why is this ministry as important to fund as another one? What do you intend to do with the ministry? Chapter 5 will help you think through how to approach these conversations.

Take them on a field trip. What church in your area is already doing a special needs ministry? Go on a "snoop trip" where you take a tour, meet some of the teachers and leaders, and hear firsthand what the benefits are for the church.

Bring someone with you. If you've got 15 minutes to present your case to your pastor or a church board, why not bring a family along that has a child with special needs? Ask the family to use half the time explaining what they need, and you take the rest of the time describing a program that would meet those needs.

Provide a dose of reality. Invite a family affected by disability to evaluate your existing program. Share that family's evaluation with your leaders. It's very possible your church leadership doesn't have a clue how your programs work—or don't work—for special needs families. We all like to know how we're doing; if you flunk the evaluation, say so and offer several recommendations on how to pass it the next time.

How you educate your leaders depends on who they are—and how they learn. But it's generally true that you'll see little change until you demonstrate there's a real need and your leaders discover that need. A media presentation will never be as effective as providing an emotional connection with living, breathing children and families who want to see a program happen.

Invite a family affected by disability to evaluate your existing program.

☑ **Check** your motives

What's your personal view of children with special needs?

I ask that question because it gets to your motivation. If you're motivated by pity, your ministry will be short-lived. You won't have the passion or vision to see it through.

If you're motivated by guilt, you'll run out of steam even more quickly. Why? Because once you've pulled together a program, your guilt will be gone. And with it will go your motivation to work through all the logistics and issues that surround special needs ministry.

If you're motivated by the need your own child has for appropriate programming—if you're the parent of a child with special needs—recognize that you'll probably be involved for a limited amount of time. When your child moves into another group, you'll most likely leave the ministry. God can still work through you while you're here in a powerful way, but be mindful to build a strong leadership team that can carry on when you leave.

The only motivation that will sustain you long-term is love. Love for children. Love for their families. Love for sharing the gospel. Love for serving others.

And along with motivation, there's another question to ask yourself and others who might join you in a special needs ministry. It's this: What do you think about people with special needs?

Thomas Orrin Bentz, author of *Theology in Disability*, believes Christians are nearsighted regarding special needs ministry. He writes, "Theology not only deals with disability. Theology is disability. It is the impossible science of the supernatural, the search for the 'law of God,' the knowing of the unknowable, trying to see the infinite through our nearsighted lenses."

Babies born with physical and mental limitations aren't a mistake of nature—they're a new means of approaching grace.

Here's my point: God's image is sometimes revealed in 20 perfect, little fingers and toes. At other times, it's seen in tiny, twisted limbs and bright, crooked smiles. Babies born with physical and mental limitations aren't a mistake of nature—they're a new means of approaching grace.

Do you believe that God can be in the creation of a child who's born without the ability to ever walk? or speak? or move beyond the abilities of a 3-year-old to experience the world?

Like all children, those with severe disabilities want to know they have value and purpose. They're limited, but not without potential. The world may abort them or shut them away; some churches may marginalize them. But God lifts them to places of honor. As we work with children and adults with special needs, we must think of them as full brothers and sisters in the Lord, not people who are less than us.

☑ **Check** your vision

People don't jump in and help programs; they help people. And they don't sign on for programs that seem to have a small impact.

Be intentional about connecting your vision for a special needs program with the larger mission and purpose of your church.

Is your church mission-minded? Present your ministry as a mission outreach to a population of people who often don't find a place in the church because the congregation doesn't reach out to them.

Is your church outreach-oriented? Present your ministry as just that: an outreach program that will meet critical needs in the community.

Is your church one that values following Jesus' example? You couldn't find a ministry that more closely shows Jesus' heart for people.

Jesus' Heart for People With Special Needs

There's nothing in how Jesus responded to people with disabilities that indicates he esteemed them any less than the healthy crowds that surrounded him. Reading through the Gospels, it's easy to see that Jesus didn't turn away those with physical or intellectual needs, ridicule them, or suggest they were incapable of discipleship and service.

Consider the way Jesus responded to these people with disabilities…

- He welcomed and healed the lepers, the sickest of the sick and the likely most disfigured (Matthew 8:1-4; Luke 17:11-19).
- He gave his undivided attention to the deaf-mute man, then touched and healed him (Mark 7:31-37).
- He gave purpose, hope, and healing to a blind man (John 9:1-41).
- In the presence of religious persecution, he healed a man's crippled hand (Luke 6:6-11).

Jesus engaged people with disabilities. He touched them, spoke with them, ministered to them. He had a vision for them that didn't rely on their being whole and healed before they had value.

Jesus did heal people—but he didn't heal everyone with disabilities. There were certainly people in Jerusalem who were still lame when Jesus ended his ministry on Earth. Jesus could have simply waved a hand and healed every leper on Earth—but he didn't. He could have restored sight to all unseeing eyes, prayed strength into all bent, twisted legs and ankles—but he didn't.

Why not? He had the power, and he certainly had the compassion.

Perhaps it's because from an eternal perspective what matters more is the condition of the heart, not how well someone can walk.

Kathleen Deyer Bolduc writes this regarding her son's disability: "The pain I experienced as I grieved Joel's disability broke open the Scriptures for me. I came to understand that Jesus turns upside down the cultural belief that brokenness is to be avoided at all costs. Christ challenged me to face and embrace my brokenness as well as Joel's brokenness, so that God's power might be released within both of us."

Of the miracles Jesus performed in the Gospels, nearly two-thirds were done to assist people who had physical needs. As hurting people cried out to Jesus, he responded compassionately. And he's still responding—through us.

Jesus had a deep, unceasing affection for people who were hurting. The Bible says 12 times he was "moved by compassion" or he had "compassion on them." He also honored the faith of family and friends who brought their suffering loved ones to him. Jesus never drew back in revulsion at the sight of a person who had special needs. He never shook his head and referred them to a clinic or center for help. He saw no hopeless cases. Jesus' vision for men and women with disabilities didn't include them being less valuable because of their special needs. Prayerfully consider the compassion and respect Jesus demonstrated in the following passages.

Mark 1:40-45

A man with leprosy came and knelt in front of Jesus, begging to be healed. "If you are willing, you can heal me and make me clean," he said.

Moved with compassion, Jesus reached out and touched him. "I am willing," he said. "Be healed!" Instantly the leprosy disappeared, and the man was healed. Then Jesus sent him on his way with a stern warning: "Don't tell anyone about this. Instead, go to the priest and let him examine you. Take along the offering required in the law of Moses for those who have been healed of leprosy. This will be a public testimony that you have been cleansed."

But the man went and spread the word, proclaiming to everyone what had happened. As a result, large crowds soon surrounded Jesus, and he couldn't publicly enter a town anywhere. He had to stay out in the secluded places, but people from everywhere kept coming to him.

Luke 5:17-26

One day while Jesus was teaching, some Pharisees and teachers of religious law were sitting nearby. (It seemed that these men showed up from every village in all Galilee and Judea, as well as from Jerusalem.) And the Lord's healing power was strongly with Jesus.

Some men came carrying a paralyzed man on a sleeping mat. They tried to take him inside to Jesus, but they couldn't reach him because of the crowd. So they went up to the roof and took off some tiles. Then they lowered the sick man on his mat down into the crowd, right in front of Jesus. Seeing their faith, Jesus said to the man, "Young man, your sins are forgiven."

But the Pharisees and teachers of religious law said to themselves, "Who does he think he is? That's blasphemy! Only God can forgive sins!"

Jesus knew what they were thinking, so he asked them, "Why do you question this in your hearts? Is it easier to say 'Your sins are forgiven,' or 'Stand up and walk'? So I will prove to you that the Son of Man has the authority on earth to forgive sins." Then Jesus turned to the paralyzed man and said, "Stand up, pick up your mat, and go home!"

And immediately, as everyone watched, the man jumped up, picked up his mat, and went home praising God. Everyone was gripped with great wonder and awe, and they praised God, exclaiming, "We have seen amazing things today!"

John 5:1-9

Afterward Jesus returned to Jerusalem for one of the Jewish holy days. Inside the city, near the Sheep Gate, was the pool of Bethesda, with five covered porches. Crowds of sick people—blind, lame, or paralyzed—lay on the porches. One of the men lying there had been sick for thirty-eight years. When Jesus saw him and knew he had been ill for a long time, he asked him, "Would you like to get well?"

"I can't, sir," the sick man said, "for I have no one to put me into the pool when the water bubbles up. Someone else always gets there ahead of me."

Jesus told him, "Stand up, pick up your mat, and walk!"

Instantly, the man was healed! He rolled up his sleeping mat and began walking!

Mark 8:22-26

When they arrived at Bethsaida, some people brought a blind man to Jesus, and they begged him to touch the man and heal him. Jesus took the blind man by the hand and led him out of the village. Then, spitting on the man's eyes, he laid his hands on him and asked, "Can you see anything now?"

The man looked around. "Yes," he said, "I see people, but I can't see them very clearly. They look like trees walking around."

Then Jesus placed his hands on the man's eyes again, and his eyes were opened. His sight was completely restored, and he could see everything clearly. Jesus sent him away, saying, "Don't go back into the village on your way home."

Matthew 9:1-8

Jesus climbed into a boat and went back across the lake to his own town. Some people brought to him a paralyzed man on a mat. Seeing their faith, Jesus said to the paralyzed man, "Be encouraged, my child! Your sins are forgiven."

But some of the teachers of religious law said to themselves, "That's blasphemy! Does he think he's God?"

Jesus knew what they were thinking, so he asked them, "Why do you have such evil thoughts in your hearts? Is it easier to say 'Your sins are forgiven,' or 'Stand up and walk'? So I will prove to you that the Son of Man has the authority on earth to forgive sins." Then Jesus turned to the paralyzed man and said, "Stand up, pick up your mat, and go home!"

And the man jumped up and went home! Fear swept through the crowd as they saw this happen. And they praised God for sending a man with such great authority.

Does Your Vision Reflect Jesus' Vision?

Jesus never excluded or marginalized the people with disabilities. Decide now what vision you'll communicate about serving these friends. Think through how that vision will be heard by your church leadership and the congregation at large. Determine the ways that a special needs ministry will advance the goals and mission of your church.

You must be able to communicate your vision clearly and powerfully. It's essential if you're going to build an effective ministry.

☑ **Check** to see what's stopping you

What obstacles stand in your way? Maybe it's a lack of time, an uncertainty about exactly what to do next, or a desire to see if anyone else will get involved and take the reins.

The Action Assessment Line introduced earlier might give you some powerful clues and insights as to what's stopping your church from embracing a special needs ministry. How well are you moving from conviction to value to ownership to action? What's stopping the process may be a lack of understanding or a perceived lack of resources.

I'll tell you what it isn't—it isn't a lack of caring. I've yet to meet a pastor who wants to deliberately keep special needs families away from church. I've yet to meet a children's pastor who truly wants children with spina bifida, cerebral palsy, or ADD to stay home on Sunday morning watching cartoons.

The make-or-break challenge is usually that there's simply not enough energy to make a special needs ministry happen.

Ellen, a children's pastor in Oregon, told me, "We don't have a special needs ministry because I can't keep up with all I have to do now. I have 250 children and 80 teachers every Sunday morning. I have to make sure everything is up and running, and our classrooms are overcrowded."

Leaders like Ellen are exhausted. "I get paid for 30 hours a week and work 50. I'm a single mom with four kids. I make 60 phone calls a month to get volunteers. One Sunday I taught in Trevor's classroom. He has autism and I had to bolt the door just to keep him from running down the hall. It's a big job to work with Trevor, and volunteers are not prepared. I'd love to do more, but it's impossible to add one more thing."

"I'd love to do more, but it's impossible to add one more thing."

Ellen's right: There's always one more thing to do in children's ministry. The job is never really finished.

Are you the person to launch or expand the special needs ministry at your church? Or might you be the one who will put this book into the hands of the person who *is* the right person? One or the other, I hope so.

Moving ahead can literally redeem lives. It will almost certainly improve them. Consider what I discovered when I talked with LuAnn Ruoss, Director of the Special Needs Ministry at First Presbyterian Church in Bakersfield, California. She shared some harsh realities about life as a person with special needs.

Pat: LuAnn, you see young people who are developmentally delayed trying to live on their own. What challenges do they face?

LuAnn: Many of them try to get menial jobs to supplement their Social Security checks. They're taught life skills to help them handle money, hygiene, and household duties. Some live together in apartments and others in group homes. Because they are free to come and go as they choose, it's easy for them to become overwhelmed with too many choices.

Pat: That sounds exciting but a little scary, too. Do most of them succeed?

LuAnn: Success for these young people is difficult, especially in relationships. The state tells them that they can make choices to use condoms or not during sexual relations. The state doesn't teach them about abstinence. Sometimes they make friends with people who abuse them and take advantage of their mental capacity.

Pat: That's terrible. Does it happen a lot?

LuAnn: I'm afraid it does. At the beginning of the month, when paychecks are mailed out, they have lots of friends. Some drink and party together until the money runs out. Friends without disabilities tell sad stories and ask for money. One girl made a friend's car payment because the friend let her ride in the car. In the end, adults with special needs are very lonely.

Pat: It sounds more like abuse than friendship. Can't something be done about that?

LuAnn: It's clearly abuse. People with disabilities are often victimized and become very untrusting of people in general.

Pat: Is that when they turn to the church?

LuAnn: Sadly, at church many of them are not invited to be part of the group. My heart goes out to them because instead of breaking the long cycle of loneliness, churches add to their confusion.

Pat: How is it different at your church?

LuAnn: We intentionally reach out to people of all ages. Adults with developmental disorders go to Sunday school classes and are welcomed into membership. They serve as ushers and greeters. I visit group homes and connect them with the regional center for individuals with disabilities and Heart Connection, a support group sponsored by our church. We offer a conference locally that trains our church members to understand the needs of these precious young adults.

Pat: Can you share some success stories?

LuAnn: I love to talk about my friends.

David, a 40-year-old man with severe learning disabilities, was raised in church. For many years he could not work full time and was not involved in church. When David joined our ministry, we began giving him leadership roles that challenged him. As a result, he started work on his associate degree and secured a full-time job counseling others with disabilities at a community center. David went from working as a part-time dishwasher to a Bible study leader who enjoys going to Promise Keepers with the men in our church.

Mary suffered with mental illness for years. With lots of love, Mary slowly changed from someone who didn't feel safe at Sunday school to a mentor for new members in her class. Now, instead of just sitting quietly, Mary freely participates when asked. It's a joy watching her grow in the Lord.

When I first started our special needs class several years ago, Robert was part of the original group. He had attended church since he was a teenager, but he wouldn't pray out loud. As his relationship grew with God and others, his mom's health began to deteriorate. Robert requested prayer for her, but didn't pray for three years. He said he didn't know how. Imagine our surprise when one day Robert volunteered to lead prayer time and simply began talking to God. I know God listens to Robert and answers his prayers.

Pat: What do you teach people with limited understanding about God?

LuAnn: It's too easy to say that people with intellectual disabilities will all go to heaven, so there's no need to worry about what they understand. I've watched them come to a personal knowledge of Jesus Christ.

One spring I asked my class what Easter meant to them. They talked about new clothes, candy, and going out to dinner. The next year, my husband and I created a hands-on lesson to teach the Easter story. We brought in blocks of wood and different-sized nails. They loved pounding the nails into the blocks and making a lot of noise. Then we brought in a wooden cross and three huge spikes. As they started swinging their hammers, Joe, a member of our class, stopped.

He said, "Is that the sound Jesus heard when they nailed him to the cross?" I nodded my head yes. All the color drained from Joe's face.

He put down his hammer and tried to push the nails in with his hands. The harsh sounds stopped as other students followed his lead. Soon the room was quiet. Finally, the message was real for them. Now when you ask them about Easter, they talk about how Jesus Christ died for them.

Today, there are more training opportunities for disability ministry volunteers than ever before. Christian education conferences are including special tracks to serve children with special needs. Several denominations have created special needs departments and hired experienced directors to serve churches seeking help in launching special needs programs. And more publishers are creating an ever-increasing supply of resources to help support your staff and help you train the people who'll make your ministry happen. Websites and blogs now contain an abundance of information to answer your questions and inspire your success. See Chapter 6 for a list of these resources.

Dr. Jim Pierson has been fighting the good fight for establishing special needs ministries for more than 30 years. In Chapter 5, you'll find his advice on how to take your request to launch a special needs ministry to your church leadership.

But before you continue reading, pause for a moment and reflect on the "Just for You" devotion on the following page. You're stepping forward to do important work for the kingdom—it's important you do so prayerfully.

Just for you

When four friends brought their crippled friend to Jesus, they ran into obstacles. The crowd was too thick. The doorway was blocked. They couldn't get in.

But they wouldn't be stopped. They carried their friend to the roof and created a skylight that the homeowner certainly didn't approve of. And their friend was able to get to Jesus.

You're one of those special friends. You're helping carve a path for special needs friends in your community to make their way to church—toward fellowship and toward Jesus.

God bless you for your compassion, energy, and love.

Dear God,

Bless the journey of our church's special needs ministry. In all ways, at all times, we ask you to provide the guidance we need.

In Jesus' name, amen.

4

CASE STUDIES: SPECIAL NEEDS MINISTRIES IN REAL CHURCHES

by Louise Tucker Jones

As I speak with special needs ministries directors across the country, I'm amazed at the creative ways they build their ministries. Each ministry takes on a unique design, shaped to meet the needs of a particular area or church.

I applaud all efforts to minister to individuals with disabilities. I recently heard a report on the radio that said only a small number of churches provide intentional programming for this population of people. I believe that is true, but more churches are realizing there is a growing need.

Following are programs that are making a difference in local churches. Perhaps the program you have—or will be launching—resembles one of them.

How special needs ministries look in different churches

Sue Lindahl, who has a background in special education and was a missionary, was the first full-time director of the special needs ministries department at Stonebriar Community Church in Frisco, Texas. Sue's experience provided great credibility when presenting needs at staff meetings.

Now in its 13th year, the program continues to emphasize inclusion and serves children from birth through high school. Each child gets a buddy to help in the regular classroom. And for those medically fragile children who can't attend a regular class, the ministry has special classrooms available, along with on-call nurses and volunteers.

Sue's philosophy of serving was always "One child at a time, and we'll do whatever it takes to meet each child's needs." Stonebriar Community Church offered the community's first one-night-a-month respite program in their city. It was called FunZone and served students with disabilities attending their church, along with their siblings. Volunteers were seldom hard to find because Sue had high standards and found that, remarkably, the more she expected from her volunteers, the more motivated people were to be involved.

Stonebriar Community Church hosted an annual "Fun Day" for families affected by disability in the community. They now also enjoy sharing their state-of-the-art special needs playground. For more information on this growing ministry, visit their website at stonebriar.org/get-connected/special-needs.

• • •

Harvest Bible Chapel in Rolling Meadows, Illinois, has a membership of more than 6,000 people and three worship services. It also has two distinct special needs ministries. The first ministry reaches out to individuals who are deaf and hearing-impaired. There is a sign language interpreter in the second worship service, and classes in American Sign Language are offered regularly to people in the church so that they may communicate with the deaf community.

The second ministry, "In His Image," is a program designed for adults with special needs. The class enjoys the opening and music of the third worship service and then attends a Bible study program geared especially for their needs. Children with special needs are mainstreamed weekly into regular classrooms with one-on-one aides. You can visit Harvest Bible Chapel's website at harvestrollingmeadows.org.

Birthing a ministry

The Second Baptist Church in Houston, Texas, began its special needs ministry program called Promise Land in 2004, which was geared to first- through fifth-graders. Children went to Bible study groups the first hour and then attended Promise Land during the worship time. During the first year, the ministry constantly adapted Promise Land to meet needs. "When we started, the ministry was more of a care ministry," says Julie Dautrich, the preschool director, who also oversees the special needs program. "In recent years, we've worked hard to structure our teaching to tailor the lesson to each child's need. We've also learned to come alongside kids with autism to better manage their behaviors in class. These children are now exposed to teaching that includes lots of tactile stimulation. And our program is still growing."

Some leaders like Rachel get tossed into the deep end of the pool, while others wade in gradually. Special needs ministries are birthed in both ways.

Rachel Richardson was a 19-year-old college student when she started volunteering in the special needs program at Quail Springs Church of Christ. At the time, there were just three kids. But suddenly Rachel found herself responsible for the entire ministry.

When the teacher left, Rachel was appointed special needs ministry director and told, "Do what you want to do." After the initial shock, Rachel got on the phone and called every resource person she could find to help her establish a program. She even attended conferences while carrying a full-time class schedule at the university. "I'm overwhelmed," said Rachel, "but I really want to make this program work. I love these kids."

Some leaders like Rachel get tossed into the deep end of the pool, while others wade in gradually. Special needs ministries are birthed in both ways.

Building a ministry

After 20 years as a special education teacher, Ethel Evans volunteered to teach children with special needs at First Baptist Church in Moore, Oklahoma.

At first, there were only two children and one other teacher. When that teacher left, Ethel was alone with four students. But she never gave up. Eventually, the church recruited five teachers who faithfully led six children and six adults in regular Bible studies. Ethel always worked the extended session for the kids who couldn't go into worship. "I think our children need the consistency that one person offers," said Ethel. "They need to know that person will always be there and take care of their needs."

The children's program offered an Awana class on Wednesday evenings, and both children and adult groups participated in mainstreamed and special needs classes. Every Christmas and Easter, kids created cards the church mailed to a local women's correctional facility. "It's a way for them to minister to others," said Ethel. Although this ministry began small, it remained consistent—and grew.

When Ethel retired some years later, her legacy remained. Today, First Baptist continues to seek out unique ways to minister to families affected by disability, always with the goal of communicating that Jesus loves each child unconditionally.

When children's pastor Glenn Barber joined the church staff some years ago, he didn't know much about special needs. "The thing that motivates me the most," said Glenn, "is the conversations I've had with parents who told me that their child with special needs was not welcomed at their previous church. I determined right then that First Church would never be that kind of church."

Including children and adults with disabilities, the church is now serving about 27 families in its Sunday school and midweek programs. The church also provides care for children with special needs during the church-wide couples Date Night program. Glenn's vision is to build a stronger training program, to maintain manageable class sizes, and to inspire more volunteers to serve these kids he has come to love and appreciate.

A blossoming ministry

At the time of this writing, the Williams Boulevard Baptist Church in Kenner, Louisiana, had a special needs ministry program that served 175 adults and also ministered to 50 group-home staff members who attended with the students. There were usually 15 church members, along with a nurse, who taught the Sunday classes.

You might think those numbers reflect a megachurch, but Williams Boulevard had a membership of just 900 people.

"At least 98 percent of the membership embraced our students," said director Cindy Mazza, who began the ministry more than 30 years ago with two children. "We had two families whose children had special needs, so we visited each one and asked for the names of other families," said Cindy. The church then went to the families whose names had been provided and asked for more names. A ministry was born.

When local schools started inclusion, so did Cindy's church. All their special needs children were in regular classrooms. The adult student population grew dramatically when the state of Louisiana closed institutions nearby, and many adults with special needs were absorbed into group homes in the area.

Thankfully, the church was ready for the influx of new students. Already ministering to more than 50 adults, many coming from a community home in the area, the church simply moved from classrooms to the gymnasium when the attendance exploded.

"You would think we would have a multitude of small classes," said Cindy, "but the students like to be with each other, so we actually had only two separate classes." One class was an advanced Bible study for those who have higher levels of understanding, and the other class presented the Bible story in a more tangible fashion with drama, puppets, illustrations, and one-on-one help. But everyone came together for music, the kids' favorite activity.

Because of their love for music, at Christmas and on the Fourth of July the students sang at nursing homes. "They needed to give back to the community," said Cindy, "and this was an excellent way to do so."

Other activities included a September picnic, Christmas party, bowling after church, lunch at the church with recreation activities in the gym, and a special ministry day in October, when the group sang for the entire church. When the group was smaller, group members once rented trolleys and picnicked while they toured the city of New Orleans. To learn more, visit the church website at williams blvd.org/ministries/special-needs-ministry.

Create a place for everyone

I once visited with a pastor and asked if his church had a ministry to people with special needs. His words were surprising—yet typical. He said, "No, because we don't have anyone with disabilities in our church." Of course he had no people with disabilities in his church—his church wasn't accessible to them physically or spiritually. I marvel at such a mind-set.

Would we ever plant a new church without providing a children's program? Of course not, even if the people planting the church didn't have children. We'd have a program ready, waiting expectantly for that first family with little ones to walk through the front door.

Oh, how it breaks my heart to hear that one of God's precious gems was wounded by superficial Christianity.

Let's be just as zealous in providing for families with special needs. No one should be turned away from God's house; nor should we have to scramble around and offer a quick, inadequate, makeshift program because nothing is in place when the family arrives.

A friend of mine once took her son with Williams syndrome to a new church and explained Brian's disability to the children's director. My friend wanted her son placed in an appropriate Sunday school class. Surprisingly, the director requested that they not attend Sunday school that particular morning. "Let me work on this and find the right class, then I'll call you," she said.

My friend waited for a call that never came.

Each Sunday morning as the other children filed out of the auditorium for Sunday school, Brian would turn to his mom with a disheartened look and say, "I can't go, can I?"

Oh, how it breaks my heart to hear that one of God's precious gems was wounded by superficial Christianity. We should be prepared to minister to everyone who walks through our church doors, especially to people with special needs. The world is often a painful and lonely place for them. Churches like those I've described demonstrate that your church can be the refuge they need. Let's eagerly accept these families and children with open arms—and the love of Jesus.

5

FIRST STEPS FOR LAUNCHING A CHILDREN'S SPECIAL NEEDS MINISTRY

by Jim Pierson

A couple asked me to join them as an advocate for their son at a meeting with school officials. A tense discussion about new goals for the boy's education plan had reached an impasse. Perhaps to relieve tension, the principal asked the child's father, "What's the main goal you want your son to attain?"

Due to the nature of the conversation up to that point, we expected the reply to be something like, "Relate appropriately with his peers" or perhaps, "Read at age level."

Instead, this father answered from his heart: "I want my son to know who Jesus is."

This response represents the feelings of many families. Christian parents want their children with disabilities to develop spiritually as well as intellectually, physically, and socially. Because of a federal mandate to educate children in the mainstream, families are accustomed to having their children included with their age-mates in neighborhood schools. That's what's normal.

I believe parents should also expect children with special

needs to be educated in the mainstream of their church's education program. The basic objective of your special needs ministry should be to include kids with special needs in the *existing* classes in Sunday school, children's church, and other programs. Other ministry facets can be added as your program grows, such as ministry to families, ministry to siblings, and ministry to agencies serving the disability community.

You're on the front lines

Children's pastors are often the first members of a church staff to encounter children with special needs and their families. It's people like you, people who are serving children, who sense the need. Who see it up close and personal. You're challenged by the opportunity to do ministry.

The purpose of this chapter is to give you information that helps you include children with disabilities in the various children's ministry programs that already exist in your church.

You can do it—and you can do it right.

Ask for a meeting to discuss the rationale for the ministry and to lay the ground-work.

Start with a meeting

To start the process, ask for a meeting to discuss the rationale for the ministry and to lay the groundwork. For many years, I've done workshops and seminars for children's pastors to help them develop such ministries. I've learned what issues concern them and what issues concern their church leadership. It helps if you begin with a meeting in which the agenda addresses those issues.

But before you schedule your initial meeting, consider who should attend the meeting. I'd suggest this as a core group: your senior pastor, the board member responsible for children's ministry, a parent of a child with a disability, a parent of a typical child, the minister in charge of adult education, the youth pastor, a professional in the congregation who works with children with disabilities (if there is one), and an adult with a disability.

I suggest you include topics such as the ones listed below. They're often hot buttons for those who are unfamiliar with disability ministry. As you demonstrate that you've thought about these issues in advance, you'll set a positive tone and reassure attendees that your church can accomplish this ministry.

Meeting agenda:

- Open with prayer for God's wisdom and direction.
- Read Psalm 139:13 and affirm the God-designed value of people with disabilities.
- Share your plan to secure the support of your church leaders.
- Communicate your vision and plan for a disabilities ministry.
- Share how you'll find the families affected by disabilities in your congregation.
- Define and communicate your ministry model. Emphasize inclusion, which will dramatically reduce the need for space, budget, and materials.
- Address how you'll recruit and train your special needs ministry staff.
- Describe your plan for effective classroom and behavioral management.
- Describe how you'll communicate with families of children with and without disabilities.
- Describe how families affected by disabilities can also serve your congregation.
- Share your plans for transitioning kids with special needs through elementary to youth and young-adult departments at church.
- Describe the rewards your church will experience because you have a disability ministry.

Quite an agenda! Here's advice about how to move ahead in each of the areas listed above.

Pray for God's wisdom and direction

Surround everything in prayer—the planning, the children and their families, and your current and future volunteers. As you prepare to share Jesus' love with children who have special needs, ask their Creator to bless your efforts.

Organize prayer teams. Assign these ministry segments to specific teams for prayer: teachers, volunteers, parents, and children. Ensure everyone in the ministry is being regularly prayed for by someone else.

When it comes to praying for each child, ask the family for permission to share the child's needs with the person who is praying for the child…and to share the family's needs as well. Pray that children's involvement will help them realize their God-given potential. Pray that children will hear the message of God's love and respond to it. Pray that families' needs will be met, both physically and spiritually.

Pray for your volunteers. Pray that children without disabilities will enjoy their friends with disabilities. Pray that your congregation will embrace this ministry. Occasionally send notes to remind people that they're being lifted up in prayer.

Recognize the value of every person

Children with Fragile X syndrome, Down syndrome, and autism are all a part of God's creativity.

Recognize the value of every child regardless of his or her disability. These children matter. God loves them. They have souls. They need salvation. If this philosophy doesn't motivate our service, we'll be operating with the wrong motive. It is not enough to serve because parents ask us to do it or because we feel sorry for the kids or because we just want to boost church attendance.

Psalm 139:13 doesn't have a footnote: "You made all the delicate, inner parts of my body and knit me together in my mother's womb." Children with Fragile X syndrome, Down syndrome, and autism are all a part of God's creativity.

Mark 16:15 doesn't have a footnote either: "And then he told them, 'Go into all the world and preach the Good News to everyone.'" People with Asperger's syndrome, cerebral palsy, and blindness are a part of the church's responsibility to share the message to everyone regardless of ability.

A children's minister asked me to visit his church to observe a child with serious emotional problems. When I arrived in the children's department on Sunday morning, I didn't have to be told where to go. I followed the screaming.

As I entered the classroom for second graders, the teacher, her back to the door, was holding a screaming, kicking child. The other children were sitting quietly at the table. The teacher said gently, "You're hurting me, but I'm going to hold you until you calm down and feel better. Then I'll put you in your chair, and we'll talk about how much Jesus loves you."

How did this teacher know how to handle the situation? She had worked out a plan in advance with his parents and had their permission to use this management skill. She asked the other kids to be calm while she took care of the situation, and she was able to help the boy regain self-control and rejoin the class activity.

That teacher understood the boy's problems and valued him as a human being. She worked to provide the care and education he needed. Today he's a wonderful family man, productive citizen, and faithful member of his church.

Your pastor's positive involvement will be a key factor to the success of a special needs program.

Share your plan to involve the leadership of your church

Your church leadership needs to enthusiastically embrace the disability ministry. It's more than buying into a concept; it's buying into Jesus' attitude toward kids: "He said to them, 'Let the children come to me. Don't stop them! For the Kingdom of God belongs to those who are like these children' " (Mark 10:14b).

Children with disabilities have spiritual needs we can meet. Disabilities shouldn't be a hindrance to involvement in the family of faith. Your leadership needs to see every child in the church's care as a valuable person who's loved by God. Help your pastors understand that this ministry is not an option! Their positive involvement will be a key factor to the success of a special needs program.

One of the most influential disability ministries I know of is in a church whose pastor has a child with a severe disability. Similarly, one of the oldest ministries that I know was started in a church where the pastor, though not a parent of a child with a disability, adheres to the conviction that every person is important and needs the love of God's people.

When pastors see the value and become actively involved in a disability ministry, it tends to flourish. Get your church leadership on your team.

In a perfect world, this would happen routinely: During a volunteer training session in a large church's disability ministry, I was impressed to see that the deacon who oversaw the ministry was in attendance. He told us his role at the training was twofold: to pray for God's blessings on our activities and to stress the importance that church leadership placed on the ministry to families with special needs children.

Here's a rule of thumb: between 10 and 15 percent of the population has a disability.

Share how you'll find the people with disabilities in your congregation

Don't be concerned about meeting the needs of *every* child with a disability in your community. Disability enters the life of one family at a time.

Some of the families affected by disability are in your church already—you just don't know it.

I was once asked to help a congregation start a program for three children who'd been identified as having disabilities. We took time to survey the church and discovered there were 17 other children who fit our profile.

Here's a rule of thumb: various research organizations estimate that between 10 and 15 percent of the population has a disability. That means if you have 100 kids in your children's ministry, between 10 and 15 need attention. Find out who they are. And all it takes is a simple survey, such as the one in Chapter 6. If your church's survey finds a child with autism, another with cerebral palsy, and still another with a learning disability, start your planning with those children in mind. Begin with the people God has already brought you.

It's helpful to know the general trends in disabilities. They change. I can remember when children with speech problems and learning disabilities were the leading recipients of special education services in schools. Today there are more children with autism, behavior disorders, and health problems. Children are often diagnosed with ADD and ADHD (attention deficit/hyperactivity disorder). Bipolar and oppositional defiant disorders appear frequently. Asthma and other allergy-related disorders are common and require the attention of the children's leaders.

The National Dissemination Center for Children with Disabilities (NICHCY) provides current detailed information on a full spectrum of disabilities in children, including developmental delays and rare disorders. Their website (nichcy.org/disability) will help you understand some of the terminology and characteristics of children with special needs. Keep their website address handy, but remember you don't need to know all of the facts. Your goal is to get to know the child's personality, strengths, and weaknesses as well as to understand the terms of his or her disorder.

It is also helpful to get to know the agencies in your community serving the disability population. Meet the people they serve. Ask the agencies about their volunteer programs. Perhaps someone in the congregation works in a facility and could provide access. Let these agencies and their leaders know that your congregation welcomes the people they serve. You'll learn more about agencies in Chapter 10.

But begin first with the children and adults with disabilities that God has already brought you.

Define and communicate your ministry model

Develop a plan—not a program.

Start with this simple question: What will we do next Sunday morning if a couple arrives with two children: a 9-year-old boy with a disability and his 11-year-old sister?

You already have a plan in place for the girl. You'll escort her to her age-appropriate Sunday school class. But what's your plan for her little brother?

You need a plan in place for children with disabilities that is as routine as your plan for children without disabilities. Here are some ideas:

- Include children with disabilities in regular classes using a buddy, an aide, or another one-on-one person. This is often called mainstreaming a child.
- Develop a special classroom that's designed for children with disabilities until they become accustomed to the church routine and schedule.
- For the child with a disability who appears on Sunday unannounced, have people trained to assist him or her until a plan can be arranged.
- For cases in which children with severe disabilities or behavior problems attend your church, have a plan for working with them in a segregated group until they can handle placement in a classroom with their peers, or provide an in-home program.

Your plan is a beginning point. It's part of your ministry model—the philosophy that drives your overall approach to a disabilities ministry. As your overall model, I suggest inclusion. The term inclusion simply means making a place for children according to their ability to be part of their peer group.

Back in the 1960s, the school system provided special classes for specific disabilities. Teachers were trained to work with students who had physical disabilities, emotional problems, or intellectual disabilities. Teachers were all specialists in one area of disability.

Today, teachers are more often trained to deal with a variety of disabilities. Including a child with a disability in a class with peers is the standard approach. As you talk with your church leaders about how creating a special needs ministry might impact your church, you'll probably hear three questions about creating a segregated program.

If you're a proponent of inclusion, you can give the following answers to these questions:

"How much will it cost?"

The cost of providing inclusive Christian education is the same as providing it for children who don't have disabilities. If a child's disability involves expensive medical equipment, the church won't have to provide it. Children's families will bring the equipment.

A wheelchair, a language board, a walker—devices the child uses every day—will be available on Sunday. If there's any additional cost, it will probably be in the form of a ramp, a wider door, or another accessibility modification. The concern about expense stems from the days of providing Christian education in a separate classroom.

"Where do we get materials?"

Christian educators want materials to help them teach the message of Jesus' love, and your church probably provides those materials. And no matter what curriculum you buy, most teachers adapt it to fit their unique kids.

That's the same principle that applies for children with disabilities. Even if you buy curriculum that's been developed for children with disabilities, you'll need to adapt it to fit your unique kids.

So use the materials you're using now. As you include children with disabilities in classes with their age-mates, consider making the following adaptations:

- For kids with visual impairments, print a portion of the lesson in Braille. Some parents have software for this and would be happy to help.
- For kids with partial vision, enlarge the lesson on a copy machine or encourage them to use a magnifying glass.
- For kids with learning disabilities, color-code parts of the lesson you wish to stress. Use a highlighter or colored transparency to emphasize the lesson's main points.
- For kids who have intellectual or developmental disorders, provide the materials even though they may not be able to understand them. Don't give them student pieces that are beneath their age levels. Ask them to do the motor activities. Simplify a couple of activities, and have an assistant help them in completing these.

"Where do we find the extra space?"

You probably won't need any extra space if you're including children with disabilities in classes that already exist.

But depending on which children with disabilities God brings into your church, you might require a room. If so, whatever space you use for children without disabilities will probably work well. Make sure it's clean, bright, well-ventilated, and near a restroom. It also helps if the space is easily accessible, roomy, and noise-free.

Address how you'll provide staff training

Don't start your ministry without a staff-training plan! Offer good information to teachers and assistants who'll work with children. You'll help them feel comfortable in their roles and have fewer surprises.

A rule of thumb: Train teachers in what they need to know for the specific child they'll be teaching or assisting. Include the following items:

- an overview of the disability
- the diagnosis of the child they'll be teaching
- information about allergies, communication level, likes and dislikes, what prompts misbehavior, and other information provided by the family
- some basic disability etiquette (see page 72)
- basic behavior-control techniques
- helpful teaching techniques
- ways to make the classroom a welcoming place
- information about the child's family
- a written job description, including how long the teaching assignment will last

And remind staff that they'll learn a lot from on-the-job training!

From the beginning, plan to treat your volunteers right. Here's how:

- Provide adequate supervision.
- Meet as a group to evaluate, plan, and answer questions.
- Provide ongoing training.
- Reimburse expenses.
- Express appreciation—often.

Describe your plan for controlling behavior—in advance

What will you do about disruptive behavior? Preventive planning makes it easier. Start with a written general behavior plan that can then be adapted for each child. Let your church leadership know that you'll be developing the general document, then adapting it for the children in your care. Your existing behavior plan will probably be adequate as a starting point for many students with special needs.

Here are steps that will give you valuable information as you adapt the general plan for children:

- Talk openly to parents and record the results. Ask about the nature of challenging behavior. Does the child hit, bite, throw objects, or run?
- Is the child on medication for the behavior?
- Does the child receive professional help? If so, ask for a copy of the behavior modification plan.
- What do the parents do to control challenging behavior?
- Train an adult to be with the child until the behavior is under better control.
- If the child is on medication, ask the parents if he or she takes it on weekends. If the answer is no, ask for it to be administered then as well.

Describe how you'll communicate with families who have children experiencing disabilities—and families who don't

Communicating with families is an essential ingredient to the success of your program. Be honest and direct. Tell the parents of children who have disabilities that you're not an expert in dealing with their children, but you want to learn. Explain that the church is interested in sharing the love of Jesus with the child. Ask for parents' help. Create an atmosphere of caring.

Avoid being judgmental and giving unsolicited advice. Use appreciative, accepting language. If you were a parent of a child with special needs, would you rather hear, "We don't know what to do with your child's disruptive behavior," or "We want to pray with you and learn how to guide your child's behavior so he will enjoy our class time together"?

There may also be times when you have to communicate with families of children without disabilities. They may be concerned about the amount of attention their child will miss out on if teachers devote time to caring for a classmate with special needs. Some get concerned that their young child will be hurt or mimic the behaviors of the child with a disability.

One way to reassure parents of typical children is to share with them how the buddy system works. When teachers have special assistants, it benefits the whole class. Encourage concerned parents to befriend the parents of the children with disabilities who are being included. They can also become advocates for the parents and their children with special needs and the church's inclusion of them.

DISABILITY ETIQUETTE

by Jim Pierson

How do I talk about disabilities?

Use the word *disability* rather than *handicap*. The word *handicap* has its origins in the 16th century when persons with disabilities were forced to beg for their livelihood. They stood on street corners with their caps in their hands. It's not a complimentary term.

Avoid the words *cripple, slow, crazy*, or other insensitive, archaic descriptions of disabilities. Expressions such as "afflicted with" or "suffers from" lead to pity and sympathy, not respect and acceptance.

Use people-first language. Don't say "the disabled" or "the retarded." Rather, say "Jack has cerebral palsy" or "Anne has a vision problem."

When describing people who don't have a disability, stay away from

Identify places for church members with disabilities to serve in your congregation

Children and adults with disabilities who embrace faith and become a part of your church need to have a meaningful ministry. Disability ministry is "ministry with" not "ministry to" our brothers and sisters in God's family. A part of your role when you work with children is to provide avenues of service for all children, including children who have disabilities.

Let your pastors and department leaders know what sort of jobs persons with disabilities can do, and offer to arrange training programs for those jobs. An assignment in the church office, an invitation to make tray favors for a nursing home, or an opportunity to pass out Sunday bulletins will make children and adults with disabilities feel a part of the church family.

the word *normal*. The terms "typical" or "a person without a disability" are more accurate and kinder.

And please: Don't describe people with disabilities as overly courageous, exceptionally brave, or superhuman.

How do I talk to a person with a disability?

Don't assume that a person with a disability other than a hearing loss can't hear. We often respond to disabilities by speaking louder.

Don't assume that someone with speech, hearing, or physical problems has intellectual disabilities as well. Don't treat people with disabilities as if they're less gifted than you are.

If you don't understand what someone is saying, just ask the person to repeat what was said. Use a friendly, "Would you run that past me again?" to make your point. If you absolutely can't understand, use a pencil and paper.

Talk directly with the person, not through a companion or a family member. As you learn your friend's world, the communication problems will diminish and comprehension will become easier.

An energetic children's minister shared a great idea with me. She arranged with ushers to train some of the children with disabilities to assist them on Sunday morning. Some of the children were able to do it on their own after a while. And the regular ushers learned a lot from their eager trainees.

Share your plan for transitioning kids through the youth and adult departments of your church

Here is an area where many church plans break down. So as you launch your disability ministry, keep in mind that children you serve will become teenagers and, in time, adults. Be sure senior staff members of the various age-group departments in your church's education program are ready to transition kids with disabilities into their departments.

The truth is that children and adults often get positive attention and placement in most churches. However, social problems can arise when teenagers are called on to accept their peers with disabilities. There must be a plan to make smooth transitions.

Keep in mind that children you serve will become teenagers and, in time, adults.

Include youth pastors in your planning committee. Make teenagers in your congregation aware of the needs of their peers who have disabilities. Ask the person in charge of adult education to be a part of the planning committee, too.

I was asked this by a children's pastor: "What do I do to get the youth department at my church interested in accepting kids with disabilities who have come through the children's department?"

"That's a tough one," I responded.

I didn't know how tough. Before I could continue, she started to cry. Her statement was painful: "We have nurtured a boy with Down syndrome in the children's department since he was a baby. He's ready to go to the youth department. I stopped by the youth minister's office last week to talk about promoting him. I was stunned by the youth pastor's response. He said he didn't want the boy in his department and other arrangements would have to be made."

One solution for such an attitude is for the leadership of that church to articulate that regardless of disability, everyone is welcome. Then select staff who fully buy in to that philosophy. If this seems unlikely for now at your church, consider finding places of service where those teenagers can volunteer during Bible study. Or work with a group of parents who would rather create a special needs youth class than to be left with no place for their teenagers to feel a part of the church. As these alternative methods succeed, your youth leaders may come to appreciate these kids and slowly find ways to include them in the youth group.

Describe the rewards your church will experience because you have a disability ministry

Children with disabilities can become Christians, though kids with developmental and intellectual disabilities have the most difficulty with religious concepts. However, in my observation of this group, 85 percent can be taught the facts about faith on a 12-year-old level. And being part of a Christian education setting helps ensure a child's understanding of the elements of faith.

In cases in which the children's level of function is so low that they simply cannot comprehend basic facts, God understands. As in all situations, each person is surrounded by God's love and mercy. But in situations where the mental age is sufficient for learning, children should be taught in order to bring them to faith in Jesus.

A favorite memory of mine will always be Helen's baptism. Helen was part of a Sunday school program in a Christian college. The teacher assigned to Helen was a wonder. She drew pictures to illustrate the major parts of our Lord's life and ministry. The gospel lessons found a place in Helen's heart, which had not been affected by the cerebral palsy she was born with. After a few lessons, Helen told her teacher she wanted to become a Christian.

Wanting to be sure Helen understood the concept of baptism, the teacher requested that I talk with her. I asked her why she wanted to be baptized. In labored speech, Helen responded, "Be like Jesus."

She became one of the most vibrant Christians I've ever known. She enriched the lives of people around her. Her life was not one of disability but one of ability. She wasn't a victim of cerebral palsy; she was a victorious human being. Her life was evidence that her soul had been reconciled by the salvation made possible by Jesus, God's Son.

Helen died unexpectedly of pneumonia. A few days after her burial, her mother gave me the set of pictures the teacher had drawn to explain God's plan of reconciling the soul. As I looked through the pictures and lesson plans, I rejoiced. Helen's wheelchair and communication devices were no longer needed. Her soul, freed from her flawed body, had returned to its Creator.

Just for you

Wouldn't it be great if everyone in the world saw things the same way we do? That because we see a critical need for a special needs ministry, everyone else sees it, too?

Life's not always like that. It can be difficult to patiently explain the need, moving forward in baby steps instead of huge leaps and bounds.

- You want to meet now—the board schedules you on next month's agenda.
- You can picture a ministry reaching hundreds—the room you have can accommodate six.
- You see nothing but potential—the Christian education committee sees a long list of potential problems.

As you meet with leaders and talk with volunteers, you're making progress—even if it doesn't always feel that way. You're demonstrating by example that a special needs ministry is necessary. As you interact with a gentle persistence, you're demonstrating that the ministry is in good hands.

Be patient. Allow God time to work in other hearts, too.

Dear God,

Thank you for a vision and passion for special needs ministry. Please kindle that same vision and passion in others' hearts.

In Jesus' name, amen.

6

GETTING THE WORD OUT ABOUT YOUR SPECIAL NEEDS MINISTRY

by Pat Verbal

When it comes to informing and inspiring others about your special needs ministry, you've really got three target audiences. You'll need to craft messages to reach each group, and one message does not fit all.

Your three target audiences are

- your church leadership,
- your church membership, and
- your community.

In Chapter 5, Jim Pierson discussed crafting messages for your church leadership team. He identifies issues they care about and suggested proactive ways to provide the kind of information they need.

There are great rewards in communicating clearly and often with your church staff team. As you keep them briefed, you'll provide the knowledge and language they'll use to tell others what your disability ministry is doing and why. They'll know what to say to families they meet who can benefit from special needs programs. Leaders are vitally important for many reasons, including:

You want your leaders' blessings and prayers. Your pastors and church board members must understand the Luke 14:21, 23 mandate that says we are to go out quickly and invite people affected by disability to fill the house of God. The heart of our ministry is to welcome those with special needs and to prayerfully support them in practical and budgetary ways.

Leaders can open doors. You may need room for a special class, but every square inch of the church building is already taken. A timely word from a trusted leader can often rearrange facility spaces. You want this influence working for you, not against you.

As the leadership goes, so goes the congregation. Have you ever noticed how programs that leaders value tend to be the ones that get spoken about from the pulpit, highlighted during announcements, and endorsed and encouraged in board meetings? Help your leadership discover the importance of your special needs ministry, and they'll help you spread the word to the congregation and your community at large.

Involving your leadership can bring about dramatic results

"I had no idea what families of children with special needs go through."

Pastor Brian Funk, formerly of Manor Church in Lancaster, Pennsylvania, agrees because one special needs program left a major impact on him personally—and professionally.

"The summer of 2000 changed my life and ministry," says Funk. "I was invited to serve as pastor of the week at a Joni and Friends Family Retreat in Spruce Lake." The retreat brought together families affected by disability for a week of fun activities. This was a group that Funk hadn't specifically served before.

"My children, Chadd and Emily, were apprehensive about being there, but my wife, Roanne, and I were blown away," he said. "I had no idea what families of children with special needs go through. The Lord touched our hearts, and we returned to our church knowing we had to do something to help."

After some preliminary groundwork, Funk formed a task force to determine what steps the church should take to become a disability-friendly congregation. To introduce the new ministry to his church, he invited Doug Mazza, now president and chief operating officer of Joni and Friends, to speak during a Disability Awareness Sunday. Much of the planning was done by people affected by disabilities. Eventually their church's deacon board included a man who is a quadriplegic and his wife.

Two years later, the church sent a team of 20 young people to work at the Joni and Friends Family Retreat. "Our church 'adopted' families from the retreat and maintained contact," said Funk. "Ten members of our congregation even traveled to Maryland to give a surprise birthday party for a boy with cerebral palsy."

Not all pastors will bond so thoroughly with a special needs ministry. But it does happen, and great things can come because of it.

Now-retired pastor Chris Spoor of Living Springs Community Church in Glenwood, Illinois, is a good example of the value of leadership. His church launched its special needs ministry in 2002 as the congregation designed a new facility. Lori Swartwout—the mom of a child with Down syndrome—became the first director. She was thrilled when the new building met the ADA requirements and had an elevator, handicap restrooms, wide halls, and even a ramp on one side of the platform up front in the worship area. When Lori initially asked for volunteers willing to attend training classes, she was amazed that 23 people immediately volunteered. And Pastor Spoor encouraged her new team every step of the way.

The church's special needs ministry was launched as the congregation was designing a new facility.

When Lori shared an opportunity to help those with special needs, Pastor Spoor responded. For example, the coffee table used during the church's social time between services was located in the back of the room. Lori pointed out the narrow passages to the table were difficult for those in wheelchairs, so they immediately moved the table to the front of the room where it was easily accessible.

When the church scheduled a Disability Awareness Sunday, Pastor Spoor attended the planning sessions. One creative committee member asked Pastor

Spoor to consider preaching from a wheelchair, and he was happy to do it. The experience impacted his life. Here is his story:

> *I learned a valuable lesson that day. I got into a wheelchair as soon as I arrived at the church that morning. During the first service, I pushed myself onto the platform. But in the second service, a member of our Friendship Ministry team pushed the chair for me. I found that a little more difficult to accept. To be passively dependent on someone else was a very humbling experience. The church attendance increased during that season. But we didn't start a special needs ministry to grow numbers. We did it because it's the biblical mandate of the church of Jesus Christ. One of our core values is 'intentional inclusion' in every area. Some people think that just refers to race, but it also means abilities.*

FRIENDSHIP'S VISION

We believe everyone is created in God's image and can relate to God. We also believe salvation is a gift that is not dependent on a certain level of intelligence.

Our goals

- Kids will experience the joy of knowing they are of value to God and to God's people.
- Kids will grow in their understanding of God's world and their place in it.
- Kids will grow in their relationship to Jesus Christ, claiming him as their Savior and Lord.
- Kids will grow in their relationship with Jesus' church, making a public profession of their faith and participating in the church's life and work.

Ten years have passed since that Disability Awareness Sunday. The pastor has retired and the special needs director has moved away. Sadly, while the church continues to thrive, it no longer has an intentional special needs ministry.

I can't say enough about the importance of communicating with your church leadership. In Chapters 12 and 13, there are four sermon outlines for pastors and 10 reproducible bulletin inserts on the importance of disability ministry. These tools can open doors for your leaders to discuss your special needs ministry with the congregation, whether it's the need to start one or the vision for strengthening your existing ministry.

Want to make an even bigger impression? Conduct an Internet search of churches in your area that have disability ministries. Most of them will have a mission or vision statement on their websites. Share these powerful statements with your pastor and church leaders. The goals of Friendship Ministries, a special needs ministry in Grand Rapids, Michigan, are an excellent example. See more about these goals on the previous page or visit their website at friendship.org.

Ask your pastor which portions of the statements are agreeable and which ones reflect your church's mission. If you're in agreement with this vision, it's very difficult to justify not actively seeking to support a special needs ministry.

Communicating with your church membership

When it comes to making your congregation aware of the reasons for a special needs ministry, it's easy to hit the wrong target.

You aren't trying to just provide information about disabilities. Rather, your goal is to move people past fear and soften their hearts. Facts and figures about disability play a part in that process, but not the biggest part.

It's a transformation that only God can truly bring about. And it's very possible that no matter how focused your efforts, God may ultimately use someone other than you to help it happen.

How God worked through a 4-foot-tall spokesperson

At the age of 7, Taylor Garrison of Cornwall-on-Hudson, New York, became a spokesperson for children with special needs. When her sister, Sierra, was born with Down syndrome, Taylor eagerly accompanied her parents to doctor visits and seminars. She soon discovered that some people avoided children with disabilities and that other children often teased them.

According to an article in "Woman's World," Taylor didn't appreciate the situation. " 'You know how there are 10 commandments?' Taylor said. 'Well, if I could make an 11th, it'd be that we should help everyone in the world who's sick or different.' "

"We believe that God sees abilities and gives each of us a spirit not limited in its capacity to receive or give God's love."

Taylor gave informative presentations at schools about Down syndrome. She made a difference in her sister's world by helping dispel myths about children with special needs.

An even more unusual "spokesperson" was Whiskers, a wire-hair terrier whose hind legs were paralyzed when she got hit by a car. A couple at the Cornerstone Free Methodist Church in Akron, Ohio, gave Whiskers her life back by making a cart for her hind legs. Whiskers became a mascot for the church's "Count Me In" special needs ministry.

"We called our ministry 'Count Me In' for people who are often counted out by society," director Carol Tolson once said. Carol herself is physically challenged and has been an advocate for people with disabilities since 1976.

"People always say our church is so friendly. I think that's because our hope at Cornerstone is that everyone can find 'The Father, a Family, and a Fulfilling Future.' We believe that God sees abilities and gives each of us a spirit not limited in its capacity to receive or give God's love."

Churches with friends like Taylor, Carol, and Whiskers are fortunate because their personalities shine and draw attention to the special needs ministries. Do you have someone in your church who would make an equally effective ambassador? If so, are you giving that person an opportunity to serve?

How aware is your church membership of children with special needs?

In her article "Levels of Inclusion,"[1] Therese M. Abrams, mother of a daughter with special needs, suggests that institutions such as churches aren't always aware that they've failed to lay out a welcome mat for children with disabilities. The lack of warmth isn't intentional; the church simply doesn't understand.

Abrams suggests that churches and institutions fall into one of five categories, based on their level of inclusion.

Into what category would you place your church?

Level One: Institutional Unawareness

This church feels exempt from any need to open its programs to children with special needs, if it feels anything at all. The issue of what to do for families dealing with disabilities just hasn't come up.

Were parents to ask an usher which Sunday school class a child with special needs should attend, they'd receive a puzzled look. And they might hear, "Sorry, but we don't have anything for children who don't fit into regular programs."

In this case, ignorance is definitely not bliss—at least for these families sincerely looking for a community of faith to join.

Level Two: Institutional Tolerance

Children with special needs are allowed to attend events at this church, but the leadership probably has no idea how to adapt activities and classes so they can fully participate. Children in wheelchairs are nearly always cast in the role of observers.

Level Three: Inter-Institutional Separation

Children with special needs are welcome but assigned token roles. And while children might enjoy activities and classes, they aren't really included in programs such as children's camps or choirs.

In many settings, children with disabilities may be segregated from the typical children, even when integration would be easily achievable. The church tries to create a "separate but equal" setting, believing that a little 6-year-old with autism has more in common with a 12-year-old child using a walker than with children her own age.

Level Four: Institutional Support

Church leaders seek ways to involve children with special needs and accept them into the group. They are integrated into classrooms with their peers whenever possible. But either due to a lack of training or hidden prejudice, the classroom leaders' expectations are kept very low.

Level Five: Interdependent Groups

Children with special needs are full members in the life of this church. They sing on the worship team for children's church. They go on field trips and serve as teacher helpers. They see adults with disabilities serving in leadership positions and aspire to be like them.

Do a candid self-assessment of your church's procedures. Ask families in your church who have children with special needs to tell you how you're doing. How do your scores compare to parents' comments? What did you learn from this exercise?

In order for your congregation to warmly accept children with special needs, you've got to overcome some barriers. Here are some suggestions:

If your church is on Level One as an institutionally unaware church...

Plan adult-Bible study lessons that focus on Jesus' attitude and ministry to people with disabilities.

If your church is to be a welcoming place that includes children with special needs, the first obstacle to overcome is to raise awareness of the need.

Look around. You can hardly pick up a magazine these days without finding a moving story about a child or adult with disabilities. Check out the announcement section of your local newspaper. You'll find numerous community activities that support families affected by disabilities. For example, April is Autism Awareness Month,[2] October is Learning Disability Awareness Month,[3] and March is Cerebral Palsy Awareness month.[4] As you encourage your church to become involved, you'll be shedding light on the needs and softening hearts.

Plan adult Bible study lessons that focus on Jesus' attitude and ministry to those who were physically and emotionally disabled. Invite children and adults with disabilities to use their gifts such as singing, reading Scripture, and praying during the service. Consider organizing a Disability Ministry Sunday, including a worship service that heightens the awareness of disability. Invite people to share their stories about how God's grace helped them overcome their struggles. If the congregation is not familiar with seeing people with disabilities serving publicly, some may feel anxious at first. This is why raising awareness throughout the year is so important. Let the Disability Ministry Sunday be the culmination of your efforts, not the only thing you do.

Another way to build awareness is to screen one of the films listed at the end of this chapter. You might also begin by inviting children, youth, or adults from an area group home to attend a special worship service. Treat them as honored guests, and make it a time of building friendships within the community.

Your goal is to help your congregation see that people with special needs exist and that we are all God's children. You want to break through indifference, denial, or fear. People fear what they don't understand, and that includes disabilities. Fear may be expressed as cold distancing, active avoidance, or extreme self-centeredness. All the comments below include an element of fear.

- "My daughter won't learn as much in Sunday school if she's with children who are obviously below her level."
- "We're not qualified to care for babies who have feeding tubes."
- "Families whose children have special needs will be a drain on our congregation."
- "Using a sign-language interpreter in worship is a distraction to others."
- "That church across town is better suited to serve those children."
- "Teachers won't volunteer to serve in classes with special needs children."

Gently work to remove the fear or prejudice that often is behind these comments.

These comments might sound cruel or indifferent, but remember: The people making these comments are our brothers and sisters in Christ. They're members of the church. God is working in their lives as certainly as he's working in yours.

Don't react with anger or deliver a lecture. Rather, gently work to remove the fear or prejudice that often is hidden in these false assumptions.

Bulldozing over people to put a program in place isn't the best option. Those people will simply be silenced; they won't become supporters. They won't provide the welcoming smiles you want children with special needs to experience in your church.

If you're a Level Two as an institutionally tolerant church...

Your leaders and teachers need education, and nobody can provide that faster than children who have special needs.

Consider what happened at a church in Allen, Texas, when 3-year-old Wakeland Stickens showed up.

This little fellow has a disability resembling cerebral palsy, but it is mainly muscular. Wakeland had a surgery that put him in a cast for 33 days. When you get to know him, you discover that Wakeland is fast—not because his legs are strong, but because they're weak. He compensates for his weak legs with a four-wheel walker. When he rolls through the church foyer, adults step aside with a smile. Other children run along beside him trying to say "hi."

One Wednesday night, his mom Joanna found Wakeland's walker standing alone in the church gym. When she located her son, she found he'd traded his walker for a pair of tennis shoes equipped with built-in wheels. Wakeland had one shoe on each hand and was fearlessly venturing into a spirited game of basketball.

"The people at our church have been very accepting," says Joanna. "The initial adjustment was very hard for my husband and me. Our pastors pray for us and work to mainstream Wakeland into all the children's ministry programs. He's a very determined boy who loves to sing 'Jesus Loves Me' and 'Deep and Wide.' "

The Stickens family has taken an active role in the church, and that's opened the eyes—and hearts—of fellow church members. The Stickens' lives send a valuable message: "We're okay. We accept God's sovereignty and if we can do it, you can, too."

Children in the church are more likely to accept life's challenges without blaming God because they've seen the Stickens do it. They've experienced the enthusiasm and joy of Wakeland. What a shame to think Wakeland might not be welcomed in some churches.

But here's a caution you need to take to heart: This process takes time. Don't get frustrated if some church members don't warm up to children with special needs right away. It can be awkward for typical families to suddenly come face-to-face with a child in a wheelchair. What do they say? What if they say the wrong thing?

> Don't get frustrated if some church members don't warm up to children with special needs right away.

You can provide helpful transition tips for people who may be struggling, but always do so with the permission of a child's parent. There are ways to respect a family's privacy regarding their child and still help friends build relationships. You might say something like: "I saw you talking with Dylan, and you looked a bit nervous. May I share a few insights with you that will help you feel more comfortable next time? I appreciate your reaching out to him, and I want to encourage you to continue doing it."

You can also provide teachers with ideas on how to include kids' special needs that they may not have considered. Be positive, upbeat, and encouraging. Help teachers get the skills they need.

Build some adaptive opportunities into your church programming. Offer a course in American Sign Language (ASL) in the youth department. Teenagers who take it (even if they take it to be able to talk to friends without their parents or teachers knowing what they're saying!) can become volunteers in the children's area.

Train the ushers and greeters team to use proper disability etiquette. Remind them to ask before offering anyone their assistance and to never patronize. Help them develop good habits such as never startling children with special needs by coming up to them from behind or talking too close to their faces. Train ushers and greeters to identify themselves first and to be specific and clear when giving directions. And most of all, encourage them to relax and enjoy the precious children they meet.

If you're a Level Three as an inter-institutional separation church…

The chief challenge you'll face is helping your leaders move past a separation mentality to inclusion. It's a philosophical difference and can be a challenge to change.

When children with special needs feel segregated, we reinforce their feelings...

- that they're somehow unacceptable to typical children; that they're broken or incomplete.
- that they can't have friendships with their peers.
- that they're worthy only of being cared for; they have nothing to offer to their classmates.

Are these messages the churches want to send? Absolutely not!

Separating kids with special needs may seem to make life easier for the children's leaders than to manage kids with differences in one room. But in reality separation is a disservice to both groups. The key is to have a more highly-trained staff available to them.

When a church moves to an inclusion model, there will be more challenges—so there needs to be more training. Some volunteers can serve as one-on-one "buddies" with the children who require extra help. And in some cases, churches will need to create a separate classroom for children with medical or emotional issues that need to be more closely monitored.

Find non-threatening ways to bring families of children with and without special needs together.

Or you can consider this: Visit the children with severe disabilities at home. Send trained teachers to make home visits that will brighten up the child's day and assist parents in providing Christian education to their children. While this isn't necessarily a best-case alternative, it's one to keep in mind. Offer it to parents; perhaps it will best meet their needs. And what a ministry for a master teacher who wants to make a significant difference in a child's life!

Also find nonthreatening ways to bring families of children with and without special needs together. Hold an inclusive VBS, an ice-cream party, or a field trip. When you first begin, it is okay to tell anyone who's worried about inclusion that these activities are experiments or pilot programs. By using these terms, you communicate that it's not a permanent situation—you're monitoring the events to see how things go.

Be intentional about having children interact at the events. Encourage children and their families to see how much they all have in common. When the time comes to include more children with disabilities in church classes, you'll have several successes that demonstrate it can work.

One church encouraged people to sign up to help out with a party at a care facility for the elderly. Many of these facilities also care for young people who are severely disabled. This provided a wonderful activity for the children with special needs and typical children to do together.

What can you do to have your kids—*all your kids*—hang out together?

If you're a Level Four as an institutionally supportive church...

You're nearly there. All that may be missing is training—learning how to go about turning a good program into a great one. And here's something to consider: You might not be the person to do the training!

Unless you're an educator who is trained to work with children with special needs, there are probably things about how to include these children that you don't know. Even if you are a trained educator, consider bringing in a disability resource person for training. The person may be from your local school system

These recommended videos can help you raise awareness in a nonthreatening way:

- "The Father's House: Welcoming and Including People and Families Affected by Disability" by Joni and Friends. (800) 736-4177 or joniandfriends.org/store.
- "In His Image: Special Needs Ministries and the Church" available at amazon.com.
- "Including Samuel: A Documentary by Dan Habib" produced by the Institute on Disability and available at includingsamuel.com.

or a college instructor. It's not absolutely essential that the person be a Christian—you're asking that person to share information about special needs, not deliver a devotion. And the fact that your church is so committed to including children with special needs may be a tremendous witness to the resource person. Be sure to invite that person to see your program in action by coming back on a Sunday morning.

If you're a Level Five as an interdependent group church...

May God bless your ministry and multiply it a hundredfold. On behalf of all the lives you're touching, thank you.

Perhaps you've noticed that communicating with your congregation requires more than just announcements and bulletin inserts—though they're a good idea, too.

Softening a congregation's heart toward families affected by disability and welcoming them requires God's love accepted and then God's love expressed. That's work only God can do, but you can certainly assist by praying consistently and making yourself available to serve as needed.

As always, pray. Build a team. Keep listening to God to make sure you're building the ministry his way, in his timing, for his purposes.

"The human body has many parts, but the many parts make up one whole body. So it is with the body of Christ" (1 Corinthians 12:12).

Communicating with your community

How do you make people aware of the presence of a special needs ministry at your church? Where do you begin?

While you may be so excited that you want to create a television or radio commercial, don't. The people you're trying to reach probably won't see or hear your message that way—and it will cost you a fortune.

But it's a good idea to let Christian radio stations know of your program by suggesting they do a news story about it. You'll get much more airtime with no cost at all.

Be sure that every time the name of your church is presented to the general public—in print or website ads, fliers, bulletins, on letterhead, and on the church street signs—the words "Special Needs Ministry" are present. Not everyone who reads the information will understand precisely what it means, but to people you're trying to reach, the words will shine like a beacon.

The good news is that the families you want to meet are connected through special services and networks. The best way to make them aware of what you offer is to notify those networks and make it easy for them to distribute information.

A one-page flier is an easy way to communicate essential information and get people to visit your ministry's website. A sample flier is on the next page. Adapt this idea as necessary, and provide copies to group homes and organizations in your community that address the needs of children with special needs. You can also use the flier as an e-mail card to send to a group's mailing list.

Each time an organization agrees to post or distribute your church's fliers, ask what other organizations might be appropriate to contact. Who else cares about providing positive experiences to children with special needs? You may discover agencies, organizations, and networks that you've never heard of.

Attend all walk-a-thons and fundraisers for special needs in your community. Having a booth and providing cups of cool water to participants on a 10K fundraiser for muscular dystrophy, diabetes, or even to raise money for a group home puts you in direct contact with people who care about children and adults with disabilities. Become a presence in their lives.

Attend all walk-a-thons and fundraisers for special needs in your community.

By all means, give copies of the flier to any family you're already serving. They probably know other children and families who would be interested.

YOUR CHILDREN ARE WELCOME!

We believe that all children are created in God's image. Every child has immense value to God—and us!

If you want your child to grow in an understanding of his or her value to God and to enjoy time with other children in an inclusive Sunday school setting, join us for Sunday school at First Christian Church.

You'll find...

- a warm, welcoming atmosphere;
- trained teachers who'll give your child caring, personal attention;
- a congregation that understands the challenges of families affected by disabilities; and
- an ongoing opportunity for your child to make friends.

Please call Tiffany at (555) 555-1234 for more information. And let us know about your child—we want to welcome your child by name!

The Sunday School Department
First Christian Church
123 Anytown Lane
Yourtown, Pennsylvania 12345
www.FirstChurchYourtown.org

If you're unsure what your church membership knows about special needs, the following survey will be of help. Ask church members to complete the survey in the context of a church service or your church's website. This is a general survey, so it may not meet all your needs. The first section explores personal awareness of special needs. The second section will help determine the perceived need for a special needs ministry in your church. The third section explores the willingness of the survey respondent to become personally involved.

For another example of a sample church survey, visit the Joni and Friends Church Relations Department. A number of helpful downloadable resource tools for an effective disability ministry is posted at joniandfriends.org/church-relations/resource-list. The survey is on page 3 of Ministry Tools.

Because you can assume that not everyone will know what *special needs* means, you can use the term *disabilities* as well. The way people complete this survey will help you determine how disability is understood by your congregation. That's helpful information if you define attention-deficit disorder as a disability, but your church doesn't.

Ensure you add questions that will help you find out what you really want to know. You probably won't be allowed to survey the church again. Make your first effort count—draft a survey that's been thought through and provides information you can use to help make decisions for your church.

SAMPLE SURVEY

Mark "A" for agree or "D" for disagree

Part 1:

_____ I have a child with special needs in my family.
Please comment on the nature of the disability. ____________________
____
____

_____ I know of children with disabilities in my neighborhood.
How many children? ____
What sort of disabilities do they have? ___________________________
____
____

_____ I do not personally come in contact with children with disabilities.

Part 2:

_____ Our church is currently assisting families with disabled children.

_____ Our church currently has disabled children active in our Sunday school program.

_____ Our church doesn't have any children with disabilities.

_____ I'd like to see our church do more in the area of a children's special needs ministry (working with children who have disabilities).
In what areas? ____
____
____
____

Why are these areas of interest to you? ______________________________
____
____

SAMPLE SURVEY

(continued)

Part 3:

_____ I have experience working with children who have special needs.
What sort of experience do you have? ______________________________

____

____

____

____

_____ I'd be willing to attend a training class to learn more about ministry to children with disabilities.

_____ I know of other churches in our area that have Christian education programs that involve children with special needs.
What churches?______________________________________

____

____

_____ I'm willing to serve on a prayer and planning team that has a goal of developing a children's special needs ministry at our church.

Name ____

Date ____

Phone ____

E-mail ____

Just for you

Communication is a two-way street. You want to shout the news about your special needs ministry from the rooftops, and that's good. But you also need to keep listening throughout that process.

Listen to your church leadership. Listen to the families you're serving. Listen to God's leading.

Ultimately, it's the listening you do that will bear the most fruit. Why? Because you're talking to such diverse audiences. And because a special needs ministry is one of loving care—and nothing communicates that more than a genuine desire to listen.

God bless you as you listen and as you share the good news.

Dear God,

We want to do so much—and we need so much help to make it happen. Thank you that you already know who you'll be calling into this special needs ministry. We ask you for patience, enthusiasm, and wisdom—all of which you have in abundance. And all of which you're willing to share with us.

In Jesus' name, amen.

ENDNOTES

1 "Levels of Inclusion," Exceptional Parents, May 2001. http://findarticles.com/p/articles/mi_go2827/is_5_31/ai_n28891673/

2 www.autismspeaks.org

3 readingrockets.org/calendar/ld/

4 nationwidechildrens.org/cerebral-palsy-program-news

7

RECRUITING AND TRAINING VOLUNTEERS

by Pat Verbal

My passion for investing in children with special needs started in 1991. That's the year I became children's pastor at a church that had a special needs ministry.

Supervising a program of 25 children, ages 2 to 15, changed my life. My husband and I served as substitute teachers when the regular teachers were absent.

We quickly discovered that children with special needs loved doing everything other kids do, they just need a little more help—as well as more hugs, laughter, music, and fun. The class, the Royal Hearts Club, met on Wednesday evenings while parents enjoyed a support group. We were active volunteers, but we still had a certain distance from the children.

Two years later, a precious little girl with Down syndrome became part of our own family. Jessica won our hearts instantly, and suddenly the ministry at church took on a new perspective. It became intensely personal, and it has stayed personal ever since.

To have a successful special needs program requires staff. And for most churches, staff translates into *volunteers*. I'd like to share some ideas for finding volunteers—and then training them for effective ministry.

Where to find volunteers for special needs classes

Volunteers may come from anywhere, but you need to make sure they're the right people and that you provide the right training.

Two special education teachers who worked at a state-funded school started our Royal Hearts Club. These trained professionals wanted their church family to welcome the special needs community, so they volunteered to create a place for children with special needs. As the ministry grew, people who never dreamed of serving in a special needs class began to enjoy the great kids…and were drawn into the ministry.

Often it's the parents of children with special needs who are the most eager to help.

We were blessed with a ready-made, already-trained staff of professionals who were passionate about using their knowledge and skills to serve the church. Having trained teachers establish and staff the special needs ministry is only one way to get started—and it's far from typical.

The first step is to inform your congregation about the service opportunities based on the outcomes of your membership survey. This may result in a short list of people who are spiritually gifted to work in a special needs ministry. Look for any special needs professionals on the list and involve them in the ministry right away. Even if they're unable to help staff the ministry, these professionals can provide guidance on how to determine needs and how to proceed.

Often it's the parents of children with special needs who are the most eager to help. They want their children to have fulfilling experiences at church, and they're experts regarding their own children's needs.

Plus, these parents can spot an adult who has an open heart for children with disabilities from a mile away. They're drawn to people and programs that are kind to their children. Sometimes it's the friendships that form between the parents that become the beginning of a church's special needs ministry. And sometimes it's a child with special needs who creates a culture in which everyone develops a tender heart for individuals with disabilities. A ministry forms naturally.

One of my childhood friends had an older sister with Down syndrome. In our small church, everyone knew when Kathy walked in. She moved from pew to pew, hugging everyone within reach. Kathy's greetings could be heard above everyone—and everything—but no one seemed to mind.

I confess that as teenagers we were a little embarrassed when visitors showed up. Yet, as we all grew and learned to look out for Kathy, in many ways our entire church became a special needs ministry. Nobody recruited or trained us. We just did what came naturally in response to having Kathy with us.

Years later, whenever I talk to someone from that church, Kathy's name always comes up. She made an impression on our lives because her family and our church loved her just as she was. And somehow, even as a child, I understood God loved her that way, too.

Volunteers may be parents, church staff members, or people you'd never think of. However, you must be intentional about communicating with and recruiting volunteers, or it's unlikely you'll get the right people on board. And you must be intentional about training your volunteers to ensure they'll be effective once they're working with children.

Volunteers may be parents, church staff members, or people you'd never think of.

It all starts with finding the right people, so answer this question: If God sent you the ideal volunteers for your church's special needs ministry, what would those people be like?

How to find the right volunteers

Start with job descriptions.

Create job descriptions for each ministry opportunity you want to fill. Unless you're specific about who you need, how will you recognize the right person if he or she appears? It's important that you think through a number of issues:

- What is the time commitment involved? How many hours per week?
- What's the duration of the commitment? A year? Two years? A week?
- How much contact will they have with the children? Will this volunteer be a one-to-one buddy or the leader of a group that includes other volunteers who will have primary child contact?

- Will the role be one of "pioneer," someone who's creating a new class or program? Or is the role one of assistant to a trained teacher? Those two roles require very different skills.
- Will the person specialize in one disability? Two? Or serve in a classroom that includes a broad mix of needs?
- Will the role include home visits or leading support groups?
- To whom will the person report? What sort of evaluations can the person expect? What sort of training?

Creating a job description forces you to think through exactly what you will be asking of your volunteers. And, of course, it makes recruiting the right people easier because they can see if your expectations match their abilities and interests.

Although it would be great if you could pluck a staff of trained professionals from your congregation, the fact is you don't necessarily need professionals.

What you need are ordinary people who are willing to become everyday heroes in the lives of children.

Perhaps you remember Mr. Rogers, our favorite TV neighbor. He passed away in 2003 after three decades of ministry to children. I think he put it best when, in an interview quoted in The Dallas Morning News, he said, "We live in a world in which we need to share responsibility. It's easy to say, 'It's not my child, not my community, not my world, not my problem.' Then there are those who see the need and respond. I consider those people my heroes."

Move potential volunteers past fear

Remove any obstacles that might keep someone from volunteering.

One obstacle facing potential volunteers is fear. Many people are literally afraid of special needs children. Potential volunteers may be afraid that a child will have a physical or emotional need they won't be able to handle. Potential volunteers might think they have to be doctors or therapists to effectively lead in a special needs classroom.

Not true; but potential volunteers will never know unless you tell them.

Begin your recruitment efforts with an ad for your church bulletin, newsletter, or website that describes the sort of people you'd like on your team and what skills they need. If you can provide training, say so. Remove any obstacles that might keep someone from volunteering.

Your ad might read along these lines:

JOIN OUR SPECIAL NEEDS MINISTRY TEAM!

We're looking for people who...

- love and accept children just as they are.
- are motivated, excited, and enthusiastic about being with and learning from these special children.
- desire one-to-one relationships with children who allow us to be part of their faith journeys.
- display high energy, creativity, and patience, and who believe children with special needs can love God and serve their world.
- long to share God's heart and learn how to bring hope and healing to families who feel "left out" at church.

We'll provide the training you need to be effective and comfortable in this ministry. You provide the love!

Look for volunteers who have servants' hearts and Christ's love

Some things you can train people to do, and some things you can't.

It's not possible to work in or around a nursing home or hospital for long before a person can discern who went into medicine for the money and who was motivated by a desire to serve others.

Usually it's the bedpans that give it away.

Nobody likes to empty bedpans. It's a nasty job under the best of circumstances, so how much someone enjoys this task isn't the point. Nobody enjoys it.

It's *how* bedpans are emptied that can tell you volumes about the person doing the job. Some medical staff look offended and mutter to themselves the entire time they're dealing with the bedpan. And that leaves the patient feeling awful.

Other staff members take it all in stride and actually talk with the patients. They make sure patients don't feel guilt or shame about something over which they have no control. Those staff members are servants—and they're doing ministry.

Training people what to do in your ministry isn't all that hard; it's a matter of building skills and experience. But a loving, caring heart takes a work of God.

Consider using volunteers who don't attend your church

I'm not suggesting that you bring non-Christians onboard to do Christian education, but be open to using people who may not be part of your congregation.

If the parent of a child with special needs wants to help you and he or she belongs to another church, be open. Your church may have a rule that only church members can teach, and there's wisdom in that stipulation. However, you may have staff or volunteers who don't actually teach—they provide technical or medical coverage to children with severe disabilities. In many cases, they're already comfortable and dependable people in the lives of the children.

Consider what a huge help it would be to have someone like this (who's also passed a background check) in your classroom.

How to provide the right training

Once you've got the right people involved in your special needs ministry—people who love kids just the way God created them, who love God, and who are committed to serving families—you want to ensure they will be effective.

This requires appropriate training.

Training volunteers to serve children with special needs can be as simple as talking with parents and implementing their advice. Or it can be a lifelong learning process that builds your skills—and the skills of your volunteers.

But know this: There's no single, sure approach to special needs ministry. Each child is a unique individual who requires a unique ministry plan.

Pastor Rick Roberts of Trinity Church in Sunnyvale, California, shared this story: "We had one boy with severe autism and multiple disabilities. When he came to church, we had someone specifically assigned each week to minister to him. He was hurting the other children, so we weren't able to integrate him into the classroom. But another child in our program has mild autism, and other than her behavioral challenges, she was able to be included fairly well." This church had two children with autism who required two completely different teaching and placement strategies.

The fact is that each child in your special needs ministry will be uniquely different and will require separate evaluations to see how much they can best be integrated into existing classes or receive needed individual attention and care. That's why this book doesn't offer a turnkey, ready-to-go training session. There are definitely issues that are common in special needs ministry and those are addressed. But there's no one-size-fits-all training that will transform your leaders into fully prepared special needs ministry staff.

Although the training provided should be determined by the needs of the children served in the program, a good place to start is making sure everyone has at least a working knowledge of five disability categories and how to respond to them.

The five disability categories

1. Physical disabilities

Children with physical disabilities need to understand that they are more than just their bodies. That is, their bodies (like yours) are containers for their souls, where they really live.

A soul is everything we think and feel on the inside.

A soul is everything we think and feel on the inside.

Physical disabilities include cerebral palsy, spina bifida, muscular dystrophy, dwarfism, brittle bone disease, injuries, and health disorders.

Children with physical disabilities generally like to participate in all classroom activities, so you'll need to provide training that helps your volunteers assist them by anticipating their struggles and planning alternative ways to play games or do crafts.

Volunteers also need to be prepared to handle toileting procedures, which can be a lifelong struggle for some children with disabilities. Don't assume a tour of duty in the nursery will prepare your staff for this; they may be dealing with older children who have social pressures surrounding this issue as well as physical needs.

Have parents fill out restroom questionnaires when enrolling their children in your program. This information can help volunteers assist kids while respecting their modesty.

2. Autism

Autism is one of the fastest-growing disabilities in America. A study from the Centers for Disease Control and Prevention reported that autism diagnoses increased by 289.5 percent between 1997 and 2008.[1] According to Autism Speaks, 1 in every 110 children born today in America will have some form of autism, and other statistics are indicating even higher instances of autism in recent years.[2]

Autism spectrum disorder is a general term for a group of complex disorders of brain development. ASDs can impact a child's functioning at different levels, from very mildly to severely. Autism is characterized by delays in language and communication development and difficulty with social interactions.

The Children's Ministry Pocket Guide to Special Needs (Group Publishing) offers these tips for serving children with autism:

- Be as concrete as possible in your stories and presentations.
- If there needs to be a change in routine, prepare the child by rehearsing the child's role in the new routine.
- If a child has an increase in unusual behaviors, this is usually a sign that the child is stressed.
- Avoid verbal overload.
- Break down activities into smaller parts.

- Build in special opportunities to show the child the special talents and abilities God gave him or her.
- Keep your classroom as calm as possible. Overstimulation can create confusion and fear for the child.
- Use repetition to help the child learn a new concept.

3. Hearing or visual disabilities

Hearing loss can be mild, moderate, or severe. Some children with hearing loss retreat into their own worlds and may also struggle with language development. Learning Scriptures is one way to encourage speech and build a child's self-image.

Train volunteers to be sure they have a child's attention before speaking. Limiting background noise distractions will also aid children with limited hearing loss. A good strategy is to teach volunteers to step closer to the child, maintain good eye contact, and use a normal voice without exaggerated mouth movements. And before volunteers interact with a child, it's important to know whether he or she uses sign language. Parents will gladly share the best way to communicate with their children.

Children who are visually impaired are often gifted with a heightened sense of awareness that helps them adapt to their surroundings. These children may use corrective glasses or lenses. In many ways they're emotionally the same as other kids in your class, but they often require a little more time to grasp lessons.

Volunteers may need to adapt portions of the lessons into large print, provide magnifiers, or copy sections on a Braille printer.

Teach volunteers to turn visual lessons and games into hands-on experiences. Instructions can involve music, bells, or beepers rather than lights or other visual cues. Kids who are blind may need classmate "buddies" to help them with new concepts or activities.

4. Learning disabilities

Learning disabilities are often accompanied by emotional and behavioral problems. Disorders affect how children process what they see and hear. Learning disabilities you may encounter include ADD, ADHD, dyslexia, and academic skills disorders. These children try hard, but struggle to keep up with their peers because of problems with perception, memory, attention, and immaturity.

Learning disabilities are sometimes called hidden disabilities because children don't look "different"—the disabilities aren't obvious. But volunteers need training that helps them see beyond the obvious. Children with learning disabilities aren't likely to sit still for long periods of time or keep track of their belongings. It's helpful if volunteers learn to create and maintain schedules children can trust and become comfortable with. Surprises aren't always a good idea.

Learning disabilities are sometimes called hidden disabilities because children don't look "different."

Teachers should steer clear of paper and pencils for these kids, give single-task instructions, and use constant repetition. Encourage your volunteers to always praise kids, no matter how small their efforts.

5. Developmental disabilities

Children can have intellectual disabilities as a result of disorders such as Down syndrome, fetal alcohol syndrome, Childhood Disintegrative Disorder (CDD), or Fragile X syndrome. These kids have the ability to grow and learn and can make a positive impact on their world.

They can know who God is and who Jesus is. Many of these kids can become familiar with the heroes of the Bible, understand Bible events, appreciate Christian music, and participate in prayer. They can have relationships with peers and with Jesus.

The goal is to help your volunteers understand that children with intellectual disabilities can indeed learn. They don't need babysitters; they need teachers who will find ways to share God's story and model in love.

How to find training for your volunteers

You may be wondering, how can I possibly hold enough training sessions to meet all of these different needs? You probably can't—but you can focus training options directly on children with special needs in your church. And you don't have to do it all by yourself. Here are some training opportunities that can inform and bless your volunteers:

Visit community support groups.

Many groups meet monthly to discuss issues that affect the special needs community; some churches host these groups. Check the local newspaper for times and locations. Visit and see if perhaps the appropriate volunteers can participate or get training through the group.

Here's a list of some of the organized support groups that might welcome church volunteers who want to be more informed and effective: Attention Deficit Disorder Association, Autism Society, Parents of Bipolar Children support groups, Better Breathing Club, National Diabetes Education Program, and the Allergy and Asthma Network/Mothers of Asthmatics.

Visit the special needs program in another church.

It's a sacrifice to have a volunteer missing from your program for a month, but if another church is doing effective special needs ministry, it may be worthwhile to have a volunteer shadow that church's teachers. This can be especially helpful to shorten volunteers' learning curves when launching a program.

Invite guest speakers to lead training seminars at your church.

Doctors, nurses, parents, authors, and special education teachers all have expertise to share. Many charge a nominal fee, if at all. Tap into your network of support groups, and ask leaders who they'd recommend.

Take advantage of Christian education conferences that provide a special track for special needs ministries.

If you can't afford to send everyone, have the person who attends buy the relevant audio files and pass along notes and information learned by giving a training session back at your church for the rest of your volunteers.

Tell the conference attendee that you expect a professional summary following the conference. Also ask the volunteer to collect business cards from people at the workshops who attend churches of comparable size or who have challenges similar to those you're facing. The business cards can be used to make contacts that will provide information—and inspiration!

Hold this training session within a few weeks of the conference. Even the best-prepared presenter will begin to forget details just a few days after returning from the conference.

Create a training library.

Make this library available to parents and volunteers. Include books and videos such as:

- *Autism and Your Church* by Barbara J. Newman (Friendship Ministries)
- *Finding Your Child's Way on the Autism Spectrum* by Dr. Laura Hendrickson (Moody Publishers)
- *Including People with Disability in Faith Communities* by Erik W. Carter, Ph.D. (Brookes Publishing)
- *Making Sense of Autism Part 1 & 2* DVD by Joni and Friends TV
- *Of Different Minds: Seeing Your AD/HD Child Through the Eyes of God* by Maren Angelotti (Regal Books)
- *Special Needs Smart Pages* by Joni and Friends (Gospel Light)
- *Same Lake, Different Boat* by Stephanie O. Hubach (P & R Publishing)

Let volunteers know these resources are available for their use, and encourage them to share these tools with others.

Announce community training events.

Many metropolitan areas have children's hospitals that sponsor support groups for the parents, caregivers, and teachers of children with special needs. Check hospitals and community websites for announcements and share them with your volunteers. School districts and community organizations often have books, videos, and handouts that can help your volunteers. These resources are often available for loan at no cost.

Search the Internet for blogs and webinars.

Training manuals, seminars, and CDs are available through many denominational and independent groups. Here's a brief list of groups to get you started.

- The Christian Reformed Church: Committee on Disability Concerns (crcna.org)
- Church of the Brethren: Disabilities Ministry (brethren.org)
- Church of the Nazarene (nazarene.org)
- American Baptist Churches, USA (abc-usa.org)
- Episcopal Disability Network (disability99.org)
- Evangelical Lutheran Church (elca.org)
- Friendship Ministries (friendship.org)
- Joni and Friends International Disability Center (joniandfriends.org)
- Lutheran Special Education Ministries (luthsped.org)
- Presbyterian Church (USA) (pcusa.org)
- Reformed Church in America (rca.org)
- Southern Baptist Convention (sbc.net)
- Special Touch Ministry, Inc. (specialtouch.org)

Encourage disability ministry leaders to enroll in continuing education.

Some would say the church has been apathetic to the needs of the disability community, but so have Christian schools and publishers. Thankfully, God has heard the prayers of many veterans in disability ministry. Schools are developing new courses, and publishers are working to create resources to train and educate those whom God calls to this ministry.

The Christian Institute on Disability (CID) at Joni and Friends International Disability Center launched a new 16-lesson course in disability ministry in 2012: *Beyond Suffering: A Christian View on Disability Ministry* by Joni Eareckson Tada and Steve Bundy with Pat Verbal. Participants can enroll in this course for personal enrichment, small-group study, or for a Certification of Completion from the CID. It is also offered for credit through a number of universities and seminaries. For more information, visit the website at joniandfriends.org/BYS.

The CLC Network is an organization dedicated to including persons with disability in the fabric of communities. Adult services and disability training and resources for churches are some of the services offered. For a schedule of their online training webinars, visit their website at clcnetwork.org/school_services.

A growing number of Christian colleges and seminaries such as Biola

University, Reformed Theological Seminary, Dallas Theological Seminary, and California Baptist University now offer courses in the theology of suffering and disability ministry. There are no more excuses for not being trained to serve children and families affected by disability.

• • •

Finding volunteers for a special needs ministry isn't just a numbers game. It's far better to have too few volunteers than to have the wrong volunteers.

You must find people who have a heart and passion for special needs ministry. People who love God and will share his love with children. People who will invest the time and effort it takes to connect with individual children and enter into those children's lives in a healthy, caring way.

The good news: God has placed those people in your churches. There are people who are capable and willing—but we must provide a vision for special needs ministry, coupled with a training program that volunteers believe will equip them to be effective.

Pray for those volunteers. Pray that God will reveal to them their place in special needs ministry.

Just for you

One thing about volunteers—they won't step forward and sign on to a ministry project until they trust the leadership provided.

That's you. You've stepped up to the plate and made it clear you're committed to your church's special needs ministry. Your love for these precious children and their families is contagious—and your volunteers will mirror that love.

God bless you for taking the lead. For broadcasting the vision. For setting the pace.

Dear God,

This isn't a ministry that one person can do alone for long. Please bring others to serve the children and families you love—children and families who need your loving touch, the church's support, and a kind word.

In Jesus' name, amen.

ENDNOTES

1 www.cdc.gov/Features/dsDev_Disabilities/

2 www.autismspeaks.org

8

CASE STUDY: THE LIFE OF A SPECIAL NEEDS MINISTRY

by Louise Tucker Jones

Many years ago, our little church was about to take a big step. We were about to add an educational director to our staff of four—pastor, music minister, youth minister, and administrative assistant. A welcoming reception was planned for Sunday afternoon, and I definitely planned to attend.

Bob and his family were friendly, kind, and cordial as church members filed through the line. The pastor stood beside Bob in a show of support, smiling as if he had won some grand prize. Finally, I was face-to-face with Bob and quickly introduced myself before spilling out my all-important question: "Have you ever worked with people who have special needs?" Oops! The friendly banter stopped. The pastor was no longer smiling as I rushed on with my conversation.

"I have a son with Down syndrome and progressive heart disease, and it's my dream to begin a ministry for people with special needs. There are many families in our community who could benefit from such a program. Would you be interested in starting one here at Henderson Hills?"

I'm sure the pastor wanted to shove a piece of cake in my

mouth, push me through the line, and say, "She's such a prankster!" But Bob looked at me with interest. Or maybe it was concern, surprise, or shock. He finally said, "I'll think about that."

Then he added what I call his "casualty clause." He said, "Every time you see me in the hall, remind me." I agreed.

I was already teaching a Sunday school class for 4-year-olds in the hopes of mainstreaming my son, but it wasn't working. Our classes were large, and I had only one assistant—certainly not enough for one-to-one time with a child who was developmentally challenged.

My son, Jay, was uncomfortable because the other children couldn't understand him. One child asked what language he spoke. And even though Jay was 6 years old, the lessons were far too complex to hold his interest. At that time I felt he needed a class on his level, where he could learn about Jesus in his own special way. And I was determined to get one.

Over the next months, whenever I'd see Bob at church, I'd say, "Just want to remind you of our need for a special needs ministry." He'd always turn, nod, and with a pitiful expression move through the crowd. After a while I almost felt sorry for the man.

One person is a ministry

After much time had passed, one day Bob met with my husband and me and expressed his common desire for a special needs ministry. He shared that his daughter had contracted Epstein-Barr virus and had gone through intensive therapy. The experience had given him a small window into the world of disabilities.

Even so, there were significant problems.

"Who'll teach the class?" Bob asked.

"We will," I quickly answered, feeling certain we'd eventually find help.

"What about curriculum?" Bob asked. "There are no materials designed for people with special needs. How will you handle that?"

Having adapted everything from storybooks to Sunday school material, I reassured him that I had no qualms about this. I told him I could adapt lessons from an age-appropriate program and, if need be, write my own lessons.

Bob's questions continued: "What about kids? Assuming there are families interested, how will you let families know we have a program?"

We did some brainstorming and came up with newspaper ads and a note to send home with children enrolled in special education classes at school. Back then, most kids with special needs were segregated into one building or room, and the administration allowed notes to go home with kids, so it was easy enough to communicate. I also knew several parents that I could personally reach out to.

Then, Bob sighed and delivered the final blow: "Even if you could find teachers, materials, and kids, the fact is, we have no room. There's not a single room available for another class."

My heart sank. There had to be something! Bob apologized. "Maybe in the future…" he trailed off. But I wasn't going to be deterred.

"How about the storage room?" I asked. Bob nearly laughed as I continued. "It's large enough. Don't you have another place you could put the teaching materials?" Bob shook his head. "Then we'll work around it," I announced. "Just give us a little corner in there to claim as our own."

"People come and go throughout the hour," Bob protested. "It's not a good solution."

Maybe meeting in the storage room wasn't the ideal, but it certainly beat no program at all—and I wasn't going to back down. A few Sundays later my husband, son, one assistant, and I met in the storage room with a cardboard box of supplies I brought from home, and we began our special needs ministry.

Let the children come

I called every parent I knew. We put ads in the paper and sent notes home from school. I was certain every parent was as anxious as I was for a special class where their children could learn about Jesus. I pictured our little room quickly filled to the brim, but it didn't happen.

Weeks passed without a single child joining my son.

Finally, we gained one more young man. But by the end of the year, our growth hardly looked like a ministry to Bob. That was, until I reminded him that we were the only Sunday school class to double its membership in one year. Bob couldn't argue with that.

In fact, he gave us a different room—a storage room on the second floor of the building. It had a window and a lovely mural on one wall, but the room was upstairs. Thankfully, our two kids could handle the climb. We continued to pray for more children.

Over time I began to realize that parents of children with special needs were skeptical. They didn't know if their children would really be accepted or if we'd still be there in a few months. Some of these parents had opted to stayed home, while others had never gone to church at all.

Vacation Bible school opened another door. Again, I called parents and advertised in the newspaper that we'd have a class for children with special needs. It was summer, and many parents were desperate to find care for their children. Also, it was just a week, not an every-Sunday commitment. We had four to six kids in attendance depending on the day.

Some of those kids continued coming to our Sunday school class, and we finally reached an enrollment of five children.

Let the adults come, too

About this time we had a wonderful young couple join our church who wanted to help in our ministry. Pam was a special education teacher, and Stan was a physician. Together they'd begun a special needs ministry in their previous church. God was blessing us, indeed!

A few months later, our pastor received a letter about a young woman who'd moved to a group home in our town. She needed a church home. Stan and Pam brought her to church each Sunday, and soon a friend of hers also began to attend.

Suddenly, we realized we needed an adult special needs ministry as well. We started picking up adults at group homes on Sunday mornings, and our "bus ministry" was born.

Space remained an issue. We'd moved the children downstairs into a tiny cubicle off the kitchen, and then finally into a "real" classroom with a table, chairs, and storage for toys, books, and supplies. It was like heaven.

Stan and Pam first taught the adults in a little house that had once served as the church parsonage. But that ended the morning that Nova Center, an intermediate care facility, brought a vanload of adults without warning us ahead of time. Many of these folks were in wheelchairs—which didn't fit through the parsonage doorway.

Thankfully, we'd recently renovated our fellowship hall into new classroom space; we eventually spilled over into three of those rooms. We had people of all ages and abilities, even staff from the Nova Center who had never heard about Jesus. God had definitely dropped a ministry right into our laps.

Reverse mainstreaming

As our adult group grew, our children's program dwindled. In domino fashion, the kids moved away, one by one, until we were back to two children.

I wanted more socialization and stimulation for my kids, so I visited a third-grade class in hopes of getting some kid volunteers to come to our class for half of the Sunday school hour. I began by asking if there was anything that was especially hard for these typical kids to do, confessing my poor math skills. Then I told them about our children with special needs who had trouble with everything—even talking, walking, and eating.

I asked if any of the third-graders would be interested in coming to our class as friends, not "helpers." Friends are equal; helpers are not. Hands shot up all over the classroom, and for the next several months, two kids at a time from the typical classroom came to our class and learned in the same way as our children.

We sang songs in sign language and told stories with puppets, pictures, and object lessons. We glued words on paper for Bible verses. The children loved it, and we gained a new child with special needs.

I figured if I could change the third-graders' attitudes about people with disabilities, they'd grow up with a different and healthier outlook about people with disabilities and positively influence their peers.

One Sunday morning was especially revealing when one of our children became upset, and I didn't know why. His third-grade friend explained, "Brian has his chair." Sure enough, when we switched chairs back, all was well. The third-grade friend had been attentive enough to see what had happened and understood his friend's speech.

Special events

Each year, we held a Christmas celebration for our kids, complete with a full-course meal served by church members, professional photographs taken beside a Christmas tree, and special gifts. The kids provided their own entertainment, going onstage and singing whatever their hearts desired. This was their day to shine—and what a joy it was to bask in that light.

Our church also reserved one Sunday evening a year for Special Ministry Sunday. On that night our kids greeted people, gave out bulletins, sang songs, quoted Bible verses, said prayers, and took up the offering. We heard stories from parents, teachers, and the kids, some of which were very powerful.

One touching story was from Lee Ann, a young woman with Down syndrome. Her mother had taken her to church her whole life, but her father was not a Christian. Lee Ann understood salvation and couldn't handle the thought that her father, who was quite ill, wouldn't go to heaven.

One day while her mother was away, Lee Ann sat beside her daddy, led him through the plan of salvation, and prayed with him as he accepted Jesus as his Savior. Her father died the next day. What an impact her testimony made on our members. There wasn't a dry eye in the auditorium, and many people's perceptions of individuals with disability changed in that moment.

Programs, problems, and priorities

Of course, things haven't always run smoothly.

Many times our ministry was omitted when mailings detailed the family programs our church offered for church members and the public. One vacation Bible school director assumed our little group would just sit in our room until I informed her that we required a place in the auditorium, a time slot with the volunteer recreation team, and refreshments. It was years before a staff person took us on as a project and our ministry was added to the church budget. Materials, equipment, books, and toys were hard to come by, and space was at a premium.

But we trudged on in spite of the challenges.

Eventually we added other programs and events: a spring picnic in the park, a fall hayride, a summer conference, a youth class, an adult Bible study for advanced kids and adults, and a choir made up of people of all ages and abilities. Our choir has performed at several churches and at the Special Olympics in our state.

We also developed a special ministries team made up of parents, teachers, special education professionals, and staff members to help manage the programs. We have buddies for kids who are being mainstreamed.

We eventually added an "extended session" staffed by volunteers for children who cannot go into the nursery or church service. One little girl was both blind and autistic, while another had cerebral palsy and used a ventilator to help her breathe. We had volunteer nurses who rotated on a weekly basis with these medically fragile children.

Lastly, we started a Parent Connection support group and opened it to the public. This group provided a nonjudgmental atmosphere where parents could air their frustrations, fears, and joys, as well as hear speakers on many topics.

Something more

The little church where our special needs ministry began in a storage room is now a church with over 5,000 members. At the time of this writing, the church is in its 27th year and the special needs ministry is thriving.

Our teachers and team members are called on regularly to help other churches start ministry programs. We feel privileged that God has entrusted us with these priceless and treasured jewels of his kingdom.

And it all started with one little boy named Jay!

Just for you

About 90 percent of pregnant women who learn that their unborn child has Down syndrome choose to have an abortion.[1] This is a staggering statistic. Until 2007, only women 35 years of age or older were routinely screened for an extra copy of chromosome 21. Now, with the new recommendation from the American College of Obstetricians and Gynecologists, physicians offer screening for Down syndrome to women of all ages.

Dr. Kathy McReynolds, a Christian bioethicist and the Director of Academic Studies at the Christian Institute on Disability, says, "This recommendation reveals an enormous, negative misunderstanding concerning what a disability might mean for a child and a family. In fact, parents of children with Down syndrome are coming together to provide a better appreciation of what it means to raise these special children."[2]

Will you consider joining these parents in their goal to be a positive voice for children like Jay who you've met in this chapter—and for all children with special needs?

Dear God,

Open our hearts to see the value of one child's influence in a church. Please give us courage to speak up for life because you created all life in your image. Thank you, that as we support families affected by disability, we are drawn closer to your heart, and we reveal your love to the world.

In Jesus' name, amen.

ENDNOTES

1 Amy Harmon, "Prenatal Test Puts Down Syndrome in Hard Focus," New York Times, 9 May 2007.

2 "Prenatal Genetic Testing and Disability" by Kathy McReynolds, Ph.D., Beyond Suffering: A Christian View on Disability Study Guide by Joni Eareckson Tada, Steve Bundy with Pat Verbal. (Agoura Hills, California, Joni and Friends, 2011.)

9

EVANGELIZING CHILDREN WITH SPECIAL NEEDS AND THEIR FAMILIES

by Pat Verbal

I suspect anyone in children's ministry would agree: It's imperative that we help children know, love, and follow Jesus. Part of that process is helping children respond to Jesus' gift of love and the call to accept him as Savior and Lord.

That's a given. We create age-appropriate programs—Sunday school classes, children's worship experiences, midweek clubs, and vacation Bible schools—to open kids' hearts to God's Word and his presence.

What's not a given is whether we believe that Jesus' invitation to children is extended to children with special needs. If someone were to judge a church by its programming, it might be easy to decide that in the minds of some churches, children with disabilities were not included when Jesus said, "Let the children come to me" (Luke 18:16).

I've seen firsthand that when children with special needs—and their families—are shown the gospel in appropriate ways, they tend to draw near to God just as typical children and their families do.

Imagine how a message of hope touches a family who has a son or daughter with disabilities when they hear about safety, wholeness, and value. Inviting these children and their families to hear this message is like tossing a life preserver to a person who's drowning in a world of stormy seas and endless challenges.

And just as there are age-appropriate and relevant ways to help typical children know, love, and follow Jesus, there are appropriate ways to nurture boys and girls with special needs to do the same. This is more than bringing the child to a point of recognizing Jesus for who he is. It also includes helping each child become a part of the body of Christ and even finding a place to serve in the church.

If we are only providing evangelism, but not discipleship opportunities, we are missing the boat.

So there is a decision to make: Will our churches include ALL children in outreach and education efforts?

If the answer is yes, then we have to delve deeper. If we are only providing evangelism, but not discipleship opportunities, we are missing the boat. Where will children who have special needs find a place to serve in your church? What opportunities will you provide?

The Apostle Paul reminds us that each member of Christ's body is important and has value. "The eye can never say to the hand, 'I don't need you.' The head can't say to the feet, 'I don't need you.' In fact, some parts of the body that seem weakest and least important are actually the most necessary. And the parts we regard as less honorable are those we clothe with the greatest care." (1 Corinthians 12:21-23a).

Through your influence, your church will begin to share a greater enthusiasm for the evangelizing and discipling of all children.

Embrace relational evangelism

My father had a homespun philosophy about life. He used to say, "Half the world takes care of the other half."

I've watched that happen. The people of God are often called on to be caregivers. It seems to be an important step to becoming soul winners. That's who we are; it's what we do. We tell others about our Jesus—one child at a time. We help families carry their cross—one family at a time.

It's our concern for others and our willingness to get involved that gives us credibility when we talk about the love of God expressed in Christ Jesus.

Remember that families of children with special needs are often already stressed to the max. Everything they do—all the activities, relationships, and commitments—are viewed through the filter of how it will impact their children with special needs.

In order to engage these families, you'd better come with an understanding of the lives they're living. And you may discover that you won't always get a warm welcome. Unfortunately, many of these families are initially resistant to churches and the message of God's love. If you could walk a few weeks in their shoes, you might realize why.

Obstacles you may encounter

Obstacle 1: The Belief That God Doesn't Care

"It's not fair," cried Joshua, a frustrated second-grader who has dyslexia. "I get in trouble for things I don't know and that's just not right." His hot tears broke my heart. In utter frustration, Joshua often says, "I'm not dumb!"

We all assure Joshua he's right—he's not dumb. He's a smart, sweet, sensitive boy who happens to have a learning disability.

Like Joshua, families who have children with special needs know that life isn't fair. So some of them figure God must not be fair, either. Why then should they worship God or attend a church that honors God? God turned his back on them; what do they have to lose by turning their backs on him?

Words alone will never penetrate this attitude. It takes patient love expressed through action.

Obstacle 2: An Insulated Lifestyle

Well-meaning moms and dads, in an effort to protect their children, can become housebound, living a "cocoon" lifestyle.

In part, the family may be reacting to the difficulties associated with involving their child in a church. Depending on the disability, transportation and care might be major challenges. So might scheduling.

Or the insulation may be in reaction to the ridicule the child has endured at the hands of others. Finger-pointing, name-calling, and other emotional abuse can tear away at a child's self-esteem. Sometimes protection from places where yet again the child can be misunderstood or mistreated seems the wisest course of action. And, sadly, that might include church.

Obstacle 3: A Crusading Focus

Some parents can become "fighters" for the cause, living with a bitter spirit that assumes "normal" parents can't possibly understand their situation. These parents become angry at life in general and God in particular. They push away or ignore relational overtures from organizations or individuals who don't have a direct connection to special needs.

These parents are crusaders, men and women on a mission. Unless you're willing to wholeheartedly join them, there's no room for you in their lives.

Obstacle 4: Sheer Exhaustion

When Jesus told us to take up our cross and follow him (Matthew 10:38), he knew we'd all have our share of troubles. They come with the territory. But crosses can become too heavy to bear alone. Even Jesus became so weary he dropped his cross. A man named Simon carried it for him (Mark 15:21; Luke 23:26).

There are few crosses heavier than watching one's child endure physical pain or emotional suffering. Multiple surgeries, endless medical tests, ongoing treatments, people pointing and staring...they take a toll as day after day parents grind on, juggling commitments and serving their children.

The hours are long. There are no days off. The pressure never lessens.

Then someone comes along with an invitation to come to a church service or a Bible study or to choose a faith that promises to demand more change, more time, more challenges. Small wonder these tired families don't jump on board. They're exhausted.

Obstacle 5: Negative Experiences With Christians

We church folk mean well, but our good intentions don't always translate well.

My friend Chris recalls a time when her son Kenny was in the hospital with kidney failure and a temperature of 105 degrees. She says, "I got a phone call at home at 5 a.m. from a church friend. I was so desperate to hold on to my son's life that I would have done just about anything at that point."

Chris' friend told her to call the hospital immediately because God had spoken to her in prayer and told her that Kenny had been healed. When Chris called the hospital, Kenny was worse, not better. "I was angry, not so much at my friend, but at the whole situation," Chris says.

On another occasion, church visitors to Kenny's hospital room told Chris it wasn't God's will for Kenny to die; if Chris prayed hard enough, he'd live.

In light of those experiences, how open do you think Chris would be to a message to join a church? Who would want to commit to a God who prompted 5 a.m. phone calls and found her prayers unacceptable?

Were Chris not already a Christian, I doubt she'd have been open at all to faith.

Obstacle 6: The Guilt Factor

This obstacle is one that parents already attending your church may experience. They may feel as if they're a burden to the church and its programs. As a result, they feel guilty and uncomfortable. Their church urges members to give time and energy to serve in ministry; it's communicated weekly in sermons, bulletins, and announcements. Parents can't avoid the tired eyes of current volunteers who are already helping.

But parents of children with special needs often find their emotional wells are dry. Sunday mornings are an oasis for them. Many of them just don't have the emotional energy to teach or lead—especially in children's ministry.

They are grateful for the special needs ministry. They know what a blessing the ministry is to them, and they see the need for more help. What can result is guilt that they're not more involved. Guilt can prompt parents to avoid church. So be intentional about letting these maxed-out parents know that you want to serve them. They can relax and be refreshed while their children are in programs at your church.

How do you overcome obstacles and reach these families with the gospel? In the same way God intended you to share your faith with anyone—through building loving relationships that give you permission to speak into the lives of people who need to hear about Jesus.

That's not to say that God can't use a crusade, revival, or a witnessing team to bring the gospel into the lives of families who have children with disabilities. God can use any means he wants to accomplish his will.

But in general, the more you understand the daily struggles of a family who has a child with special needs, the more they'll hear you when you share your faith.

Since there are few community programs planned for children with special needs, I've found that these families will attend special needs events at church even if they don't have any previous experience with the church.

Here are some ways you can reach out to the community, with an eye toward forming relationships with families. These "evangelism events" are each designed to engage and support families coping with disabilities where they live and breathe.

Reaching out to the community

Host weekly support groups for parents, caregivers, and siblings.

You'll need a place to meet and a means to advertise. And may I suggest that though it's easier to combine all three of these groups into one support group, it's better if you keep them separate. Why? Because someone in the family has to stay home to care for the child with special needs. Remember, the issues for a parent may be very different from the issues faced by a sibling or caregiver. And, of course, you'll need to have competent facilitators available. A veteran parent, special education teacher, or family counselor can often be a good choice.

Provide respite care.

On a monthly (or bimonthly) basis, host an event where children with special needs and their siblings stay at the church for the evening and parents get the chance to dine out, shop, or simply rest. In providing this much-needed break, we model the body of Christ and open the door to helping others know him.

You'll need to have sufficient volunteers and an appropriate program prepared. This sort of event can quickly create "regulars" in the community who become familiar with your volunteer staff and facility.

"Buddy Break" is a respite program of Nathaniel's Hope in Orlando, Florida. Tim and Marie Kuck founded this ministry. Their son, Nathaniel, was born with multiple birth anomalies, endured constant hospital visits, and at age 4 went to be with Jesus.

"Through our miracle boy we grew to love the special community we had stumbled into and couldn't leave them. We felt called to pull alongside kids and families with special needs to cheer them on their journey. We currently have 42 Buddy Break partners operating in eight states, but our goal is to have 1,000 respite programs by 2020," say the Kucks. To learn more about how to start a respite program, visit their website at NathanielsHope.org.

Provide a family night for churched and unchurched families.

Families who have children with special needs want opportunities for their children to make friends, play with typical children, and enjoy socializing in a safe, accepting environment.

You can provide that opportunity by hosting a regular evening of programming in which families with typical children are invited to have fun alongside families who have children with special needs. They can share a meal, play games, and simply interact.

But be sure everyone is fully informed on who's participating and what to expect of the evening. One church I'm familiar with is growing because they distribute fliers at a large school for the blind each month.

Hold a family retreat or camp.

Family retreats and camps are the highlight of many families' annual vacation. Relationships are built that change lives, especially for those who go to serve, not to be served.

Joni and Friends Family Retreat directors often hear from parents that their retreats are a slice of heaven on earth. Why? Because retreats and camps are places where the entire family can feel understood, accepted, and supported.

Your church can sponsor a family affected by disabilities to attend a Joni and Friends Family Retreat next summer. Learn more at joniandfriends.org/family-retreats.

Host seminars that build parenting and marriage skills.

The strain of raising a child with special needs can seriously challenge a marriage. Provide practical support by holding regular seminars that don't require a long-term commitment or an ongoing scheduling challenge. Books and video courses on the Christian family are available through Focus on the Family (family.org), Family Life Ministry (familylife.com), and Dr. Kevin Leman (drleman.com).

Plan outreach events that serve the special needs community.

One church hosted a spring fashion show and luncheon featuring "adaptive apparel." They worked with a clothing retailer that specialized in garments that were easy to get into for a person in a wheelchair or wearing leg braces. They invited a community leader who was also disabled to emcee the event, and 125 people attended.

Present plays that include roles for children with special needs.

Stories like Max Lucado's *The Crippled Lamb* and *You Are Special* make great plays. Young children are born actors and love dress-up. Ask your church drama team or a talented individual in the congregation to adapt a favorite story for children with disabilities to perform onstage. Invite everyone to try out, and include anyone who cares enough to audition.

Party! Party! Party!

Find or create a reason to throw a party. The Royal Hearts Club I directed in Yorba Linda, California, had an annual '50s party. At first I wondered, *What do these kids know about the '50s?* But their parents helped girls dress in poodle skirts and bobby socks. The boys sported black leather jackets with their hair slicked back in ducktails. Children jumped at the chance to imitate Elvis Presley as golden oldies blasted through the sound system. Our attendance doubled, and parents had as much fun as the kids.

Everyone looked different because of their costumes. There was no need to feel self-conscious about a cleft palate or leg braces. Certainly not when the kid standing onstage had pasted-on sideburns!

Embrace evangelism that helps children grow in faith, love, and knowledge of God

You've reached out, and now you have families who have children with special needs involved in your church.

Remember it's equally important in the evangelism process to provide places for those children to grow in their faith and to express their faith in service. It's not enough to "warehouse" children as you serve their parents and siblings. The children with special needs that God has brought to your church deserve to grow, too.

Encourage growth in the classroom

Children have a great spiritual capacity to know God, but they need instruction—just like adults. In many churches, that instruction takes place in Sunday school where teachers lecture to teach.

Lectures and talks simply won't work well for many children with special needs (or for typical children, either). Children may not possess the appropriate level of language comprehension. Besides, what children need is to feel Jesus' love expressed through relationships. Lectures don't encourage relationships to form and flourish.

The goal of a class isn't to cover a lot of material; it's to communicate with children in a relevant way—to come alongside children and encourage those who don't know Jesus to experience him, to help children who know Jesus to love him, and to help children who love Jesus to actively follow and serve him.

Generally speaking, there are several things to consider when adapting Sunday school curriculum for use in a special needs classroom:

Relax. Good teaching is good teaching for all children.

Effective ministry to kids is effective ministry to all kids. If leaders are sensitive to each child in their care, they'll make many adaptations and adjustments automatically. Encourage leaders to focus less on how they're teaching and more on whether children are engaged and learning. A learner-centered approach to teaching makes sure no child will be left out.

The book *Special Needs Smart Pages* by Joni and Friends[1] contains a comprehensive section on how to adapt curriculum, games, and music for children with special needs.

Know your children.

Talk with parents to discover a child's specific needs and preferences.

- Does the child use special equipment such as a walker or wheelchair? Ask how you can best arrange the area to accommodate the need.
- Does the child have physical challenges with vision, speech, hand dexterity, or large motor skills? Ask how to best assist the child with lesson activities.
- Does the child have food allergies? Ask what snacks the child prefers. What foods must you avoid?
- Does the child need specific help with certain tasks? What tasks does she want to do herself?

Use this information discreetly. It's important not to stigmatize children, in spite of physical or invisible limitations. The rest of the kids will take cues from the teacher about how to treat classmates with disabilities. If the teachers communicate love and sensitivity, kids will imitate it.

Ask teachers to frequently share the gospel story.

"We will not hide these truths from our children; we will tell the next generation about the glorious deeds of the Lord, about his power and his mighty wonders" (Psalm 78:4). Children love to hear stories over and over again, and we have the greatest story ever told. "Jesus loves me, this I know, for the Bible tells me so."

"For God loved the world so much that he gave his one and only Son, so that everyone who believes in him will not perish but have eternal life" (John 3:16).

Even children with severe disabilities can understand receiving and giving love. While our care and kindness shows God's love, we also need to tell children often that God's Son came to Earth as a baby to give his life so they can live with him forever in heaven. Simple pictures, Bible verses, and songs can comfort children with special needs in sad and happy times.

"So you have not received a spirit that makes you fearful slaves. Instead you received God's Spirit when he adopted you as his own children. Now we call him, 'Abba, Father.' For his Spirit joins with our spirit to affirm that we are God's children" (Romans 8:15-16). If you feel inadequate to share the gospel with a child, ask the Holy Spirit to guide you and to be so clearly evident in your life that the children will see Jesus in you. The Holy Spirit is the one who changes children's lives as they trust in Jesus.

The goal of teaching isn't to cover ground as you dash through Bible lessons on a set schedule.

Remember: The goal of teaching isn't to cover ground as you dash through Bible lessons on a set schedule. The goal is to nurture young faith and establish it in willing, loving hearts. Some children with special needs will never be able to memorize the books of the Bible in order. Other children with special needs could easily bury you in a game of Bible trivia. Don't assume that an impaired ability to see or speak implies an impaired capacity to learn.

Encourage growth through service

In the past 10 years, there has been a growing trend to involve children in service projects in their communities. Children used to be observers at church. They sat in their chairs, watching the action until at some future point they would become old enough to join in the exciting game of serving others. Hopefully, your church has discovered that today's kids love action and challenge.

But what about children with special needs? Can kids in wheelchairs be of service? Absolutely! A child with a desire to help others can do so in a ministry; there's something for every child to do. It may not be shoveling the driveway for a senior adult who's unable to do the job. But how about calling and encouraging that senior or writing a cheerful card? Of course! That's ministry—and that's service a child in a wheelchair can easily do.

So let children serve—in meaningful ways—and you'll help them grow.

Surround children who have special needs with "faith-enablers." These are the sort of adults who…

- act in ways that communicate they believe children with special needs have a dynamic faith experience and can know, love, and follow Jesus.
- authentically listen to children, aware that God can speak to and through them.
- are careful not to belittle or put down children.
- include children in spiritual activities along with adults.
- are willing to see and respond to children as people rather than disabilities.
- trust God to work through children with special needs to do significant and meaningful ministry.

What are service projects that a child with special needs could participate in? Here are some suggestions:

- Adapt whatever service programs already exist to make room for children with special needs. Do you have a children's choir? A puppet team? How could you expand those ministries to include children with special needs?
- Involve children as greeters or ushers. There's no one who can deliver a heartfelt handshake and greeting quite like a young man with Down syndrome. And every visitor will get the message that everyone is welcome.
- Recruit children to pray for staff. God listens to children! Ask children to each "adopt" a church staff member for a day to pray for that person. Let the staff member know the child is praying for him or her.
- Ask the child what he or she enjoys doing, and turn it into a service project. If children have made a faith commitment and know God, they have been gifted to serve. In what ways? Ask children what they enjoy, what they do well, what they want to do. Then find ways to provide opportunities for them to serve.
- Encourage children to make gifts for others. It can be colorful finger-painted pictures for homebound people or bookmarks for the church

library. What's important is that the project is meaningful and truly helps someone else. Busywork doesn't build self-esteem.

- Ask children to volunteer in a resource center. If you have a centralized area for keeping craft supplies and curriculum resources, let children keep it neat and organized. You may need to provide very attentive supervision, but it's certainly a significant service project. And there's a bonus: As teachers pick up supplies or drop them off, there's a chance for your kids to hear a sincere thank-you from adults they've served.
- Ask children to be facility helpers. They can straighten chairs, wash whiteboards, and clear off tables.
- Ask children to help with food. If your church has a Wednesday night family meal or a snack table on Sunday morning, children can set tables, help serve food, and make table centerpieces.
- And don't forget the church office. With a little guidance, children can help with folding or stuffing bulletins or other clerical tasks.

Evangelism is a process for all children and may take time

We like to see results. We'd like to share the gospel one time and see a child's eyes light up with understanding and commitment. But in the same way that it's often not the case with adults, it's often not the case with children who have special needs. Relationships build trust, but they require our time, energy, focused efforts, and sometimes much more.

I remember being stopped in the church hallway one Sunday morning by a friend who taught high school. Judy's eyes brimmed with tears as she told me about the struggles of her nephew, Alex.

"My sister called this weekend and wants us to take Alex," Judy said. "He's on medication for hyperactivity and behind in school. When he stayed with us last summer, I worried that he was being neglected because he was so thin." Alex's mom struggles with mental problems, sometimes requiring hospitalization. "We want to do what's right for Alex," Judy continued. "But Jeff and I have our own two sons to think about. How will bringing Alex to live with us affect them?"

We talked about Judy's fears that morning, and prayed for God's guidance in Alex's future.

More than anything else, Jeff and Judy wanted Alex to learn to trust Jesus through this difficult time. "I know Alex must be thinking that his parents don't want him," Judy sighed. "How sad is that!"

We're building the kingdom one child at a time, and each child has unique needs.

Learning to trust Jesus and developing a healthy sense of self won't happen overnight, especially for a child with Alex's history. It would require the patient, loving example of Jeff and Judy, as well as a church family willing to accept and love him.

We're building the kingdom one child at a time, and each child has unique needs. In the case of children with disabilities, those needs can be significant. In a culture that feeds on productivity and results, it can be discouraging when the attendance of the special needs ministry doesn't grow as fast as other ministries, but it is no less valuable. That's all the more reason to continue reaching out to these precious children and their families with the good news.

Remember my friend Chris?

Her son Kenny was born with spina bifida. He had partial movement in his arms, but no movement from his chest down. Although caring for him in a church setting was a challenge, Kenny loved Sundays and knew Jesus.

His delightful personality always won people's hearts.

"Kenny thrived on the attention he got at church," says Chris. "Even though he wore an oxygen mask, no one seemed to shun him. His classmates were always fascinated by his sense of humor."

When Kenny died at age 12, Chris was grateful for her church family, a family who celebrated Kenny's life.

I've discovered that children with special needs have a below-average life expectancy. They live a little more on the edge. They tend to have less robust immune systems and more medical complications than typical children. Parents of these children are well aware that their children are at risk.

Often, the children know it, too.

These aren't children we can set aside to evangelize later in life. There may not be a "later in life" for them. If they're going to hear about Jesus and serve him, now is the time.

Do you value evangelism?

Do you value the worth of each child?

How would the family of a child with disabilities be able to tell that you do if they walked into your church next Sunday morning?

Just for you

Jesus wants children to come to him—to know, love, and follow him.

He values all children. So do you. He reaches out to everyone—the great and small, the rich and poor, those who run swiftly, and those who are crippled and lame. You're reaching out to everyone, too.

You're doing the work of God. Rejoice in that! Celebrate the obstacles and difficulties you encounter—they're reminders to lean on God for strength as you serve him.

Dear God,

Bring us the children you want us to serve in our ministry. Give us grace to greet every child just as you would.

In Jesus' name, amen.

ENDNOTE

1 *Special Needs Smart Pages* by Joni and Friends (www.joniandfriends.org/store)

10

HOW TO PARTNER WITH COMMUNITY AGENCIES

by Pat Verbal

It's an annual challenge around my house: When November rolls around, I start hearing hints about how wonderful it would be to have a traditional American Thanksgiving meal. A turkey with all the trimmings—and that includes everything from homemade cranberry dressing to fresh pumpkin pie with whipped cream topping.

Of course, during all their heartfelt pleas for a hearty meal, my family fails to mention who might help with the preparations. The cooking (and cleaning, too!) is supposed to be my contribution to the holiday. The rest of the family's contribution is to watch football and compliment me on a job well done.

There was a time I dragged out recipe books and started a two-page list of all the requisite ingredients. It was just assumed I'd whip everything up from scratch, and I didn't want to disappoint anyone.

Those days are long gone. Although I can still baste a mean turkey, I've caught on that almost everything I need for Thanksgiving dinner comes either in a ready-to-go box or frozen in a bag.

We're all busy; all looking for quicker, easier ways to get things done. It's not that I love my family less; it's that I simply don't have time to peel potatoes, mash cranberries, and preheat an oven two days in advance. I want to partner with Sara (Lee) and save myself some work. Plus, I have never been able to make some of those recipes turn out quite right. I want to take advantage of Betty (Crocker) and her expertise.

I always say, "There's no sense reinventing the wheel."

This philosophy can apply to ministry as well. There are clearly times you have to start from scratch—creating programs to address unique needs in your community or church. But even then you can benefit from observing how other churches approach similar issues.

Sometimes it pays to cooperate. And it always pays to learn from others.

I live in the Deep South, where there aren't many youth groups organizing drives for heavy coats for the homeless. Any youth group that wants to put one together will likely have to figure it out from the ground up. Around here, that's a start-from-scratch ministry.

But if you're put in charge of a swim ministry (don't laugh—there are swim ministries in churches where kids go camping and swimming in area lakes), that's a good time to team up with a local community swimming pool. Ministries arrange to rent or use the pool during certain hours, and during that time, they teach the Bible lesson as kids also learn to swim. For a swim ministry, you don't have to rip up the church parking lot and put in an Olympic-sized pool.

Sometimes it pays to cooperate. And it always pays to learn from others.

Special needs ministry as a cooperative effort—a caution

Perhaps you're starting a special needs ministry or trying to improve the effectiveness of your current programs. Nobody knows better than you that you can use a little help. I'd like to suggest partnering with both national organizations and with community agencies.

But first, a word of caution about partnerships.

Your goal as a ministry isn't just to improve the quality of life for children with special needs and their families. That's a worthy goal, but not a uniquely Christian one. At some point, you'll want to present biblical truth and invite people to have a relationship with God as well as with you. It's at that point you cross the line as far as many disabilities-related community agencies are concerned.

Agencies are often very willing to work with faith-based organizations as long as the religious aspect is out of it. These are secular agencies, often funded through sources that strictly forbid discussing faith issues. Even the Christians working at these agencies find their hands tied.

When you partner with agencies, you run the risk of being "unequally yoked" with an organization that has very different goals from yours. What's deceptive is that you'll look like soul mates at first: You both care about children with special needs, you both want to provide support and respite for parents, and you both may use the same language.

I caution you to ask the hard questions on the front end: What are your expectations regarding our sharing the gospel? What about praying with people? Can we encourage participation at church services?

There are excellent partnering opportunities out there, but not every opportunity is a match. Be open about your own intentions, and ask good questions about a potential partner's intentions and expectations.

It's helpful to have already created a mission statement and defined your goals before you explore partnering with agencies of any sort. Again, the outcomes you desire may overlap but not be compatible in the end. If accepting a grant to outfit a special needs classroom in your church requires you to give up presenting the good news, the price is too high.

If you can't find local agencies to partner with, you're not alone. There are excellent Christian organizations that have experience, expertise, and a willingness to help the local church.

On the following pages are a few you'll want to contact.

▸ *Joni and Friends and the Christian Institute on Disability*

Our mission is to communicate the gospel and equip Christ-honoring churches worldwide to evangelize and disciple people affected by disabilities.

Joni and Friends' ministry is probably the largest and best-known worldwide special needs ministry.

Some moms and dads of children with disabilities feel the same way about Joni and Friends as you might feel about oxygen: They can't imagine life without this ministry. From the time their children were diagnosed with physical disabilities to the day they decided on living-assisted group homes, Joni and Friends' ministry has been there to provide information, counseling, camps, retreats, and lots of love.

From her own wheelchair, Joni Eareckson Tada has reached out to children and adults with disabilities, as well as their family members and friends, for more than 30 years.

Following a diving accident in 1967, Joni was left with no feeling from the neck down and only limited movement of her hands. In those early days of depression, Joni says the support of her church and church friends made all the difference.

"The darkness was lifted when friends from my church rallied around my family, offering help, hope, and ascribing positive meaning to my affliction," says Joni. "It was the church that kept us connected to reality, opening doors of possibilities and paving the way for me to re-enter the mainstream of life."

What would have happened if members of Joni's church hadn't opened their hearts and acted on the biblical call of Christ? Small wonder Joni has made it her life's work to train the church for effective ministry in the area of special needs.

At the time of this writing, Joni and Friends has 21 national Field Ministries with teams dedicated to "get in the trenches" with your church, providing training, mission opportunities, prayer support, and encouragement. The ministry also reaches worldwide through radio and television, as well as Wheels for the World and International Outreach. Joni and Friends radio broadcasts are carried daily on more than 500 radio stations.

The Christian Institute on Disability launched in 2007 to impact the church, Christian and public institutions, and societies with a biblical worldview and life-giving truth on issues pertaining to life, dignity, justice, and equality that affect people with disability. Once you've visited the website at joniandfriends.org, you'll tag it as one of your favorites and stop by often.

▸ Friendship Ministry

Our mission is to share God's love with people who have intellectual disabilities and to enable them to become an active part of God's family.

Friendship Ministry is an international, inter-denominational ministry with more than 25 years of service. Friendship helps equip churches from more than 65 denominations to include people with intellectual disabilities. Whether your church is interested in starting a Friendship group or continuing a long-standing program, they have tools, webinars, and resources that are user-friendly.

Friendship also has an excellent program on how to become a mentor to an individual with intellectual disabilities, as well as how to create support teams. Visit the website at friendship.org.

▸ Life Without Limbs

Our mission is to cross boundaries and break down barriers, to build bridges that bring people to the love and hope found in Jesus Christ.

Nick Vujicic's unique personal story gives him entrée with children, teenagers, and adults of all nationalities and backgrounds. His ministry is impacting churches, colleges, and other audiences and opening people's hearts to God's plan for suffering and disability. Although Nick was born with no arms or legs, his disability in no way diminishes his ability to penetrate people's lives. Almost without realizing it, people come to accept others with disabilities to be the same as everyone else, with the same hunger for Jesus and need for hope.

There are several ways to partner with Life Without Limbs. First, visit the website at lifewithoutlimbs.org, where the message is "From No Limbs to No Limits!" And this is just how the powerful stories and videos will make you feel. Recommend the site to your pastor, church leaders, special needs ministry team, teachers, and volunteers.

Secondly, show *The Butterfly Circus* video in your church to open doors for your ministry and encourage people to pray for individuals with disabilities and their families. And thirdly, consider the possibility of inviting Nick to speak in your area. It may require networking with other churches, but that's the message of this chapter, after all!

▸ *Alternative Designs for Special Education (ADSE)*

Our mission is to serve the needs of private education and parents so that there are options for public school special education programming.

ADSE is committed to serving the needs of children with special needs in private education and home school programs. Dr. Julie Lane started the company to provide support through on-site consultations and professional development, regional seminars, conferences, and virtual/online collaboration. Dr. Lane's team is comprised of professionals who have extensive experience working with school communities to meet the needs of a broad range of kids with disabilities.

Many churches that operate as Christian schools or home school organizations hesitate to enroll children with special needs. Perhaps your church has some families who home school their children with special needs because they couldn't find an accepting school. You can become an advocate for inclusive education by recommending Alternative Designs and their website at adspecialed.com.

Working with schools

How many teachers do you know? How many teachers are in the public elementary school closest to where your church meets?

Now multiply that number by two.

You'll be hard-pressed to find a teacher who doesn't have at least two children with special needs in his or her classroom and who wouldn't welcome help in making the education process a success for each of those children.

Can you imagine the impact if your church provided five volunteers per week to a special education teacher at your local school? These volunteers would be welcomed with open arms. Trust me. I've seen it.

It wasn't long before word traveled into the community that Ramero's congregation cared deeply about children with special needs.

When my friend Ramero was in elementary school, he struggled with reading. That disability had a negative impact on his school years, and as an adult he desired to connect with similarly challenged children so he could assist them.

Sharing his dream with fellow church members, Ramero recruited several children's ministry volunteers to serve as mentors in a local school. After passing the required background checks, they each had the opportunity to visit a child once a week.

The mentors met together at church on Sundays, encouraging each other and praying for the children they served. It wasn't long before word traveled into the community that Ramero's church congregation cared deeply about children with special needs. Several families began to attend the church, and a teacher from the school became a member of the church.

When caring Christians volunteer to serve children with special needs in a local school, the impact goes beyond the children themselves. Teachers who have their loads lightened, even for a few hours per week, feel the difference. Families whose children get some desperately needed attention and tutoring feel the difference, and the volunteers will feel the difference, too.

When I'm helping a child with disabilities at church, I ask for the parents' permission to visit the child's school. Spending even half a day with that child in a classroom environment helps me more than any other training. Each child's situation is unique. This is especially true for children with severe physical disabilities.

I watch how the teacher handles the child's needs. Sometimes teachers have higher expectations than parents, and I can see how a child functions when doing his or her absolute best. Teachers are often better able to describe a child's social interactions because parents tend to be alone with their children and don't see peer-to-peer contact.

I'm careful to call in advance, follow school procedures, and take notes to refer to later. I'm respectful of the school's process, and I remember to thank teachers and school administrators. Those courtesies help smooth the way for me to return later. Visiting the schools and interacting with the professionals, I realize that as with most organizations, special needs educators have their own specialized language and the meaning of words or abbreviations isn't evident to nonprofessionals. Get in the habit of asking questions and taking notes.

Here are a few terms with which you'll need to become familiar:

- *Adaptive behavior:* the extent to which a child is able to adjust to a new environment, task, object, or person
- *Assistive technology:* any equipment or systems used to increase function in children with disabilities
- *At risk:* children who are likely to have difficulties due to home or medical circumstances
- *Due process:* a formal session between parents and schools conducted by an impartial officiant to resolve special education disagreements
- *IDEA:* Individuals with Disabilities Education Act or "appropriate" educational plan to meet a child's needs
- *IEP:* Individualized Education Program written for each child in special education
- *Least Restrictive Environment (LRE):* placement of a child with disabilities in a setting to have maximum contact with children who do not have disabilities (mainstreaming)
- *Related services:* services kids require to get special education, transportation, counseling, speech therapy, and crisis intervention
- *Screening committee:* the local school committee who decides if the child qualifies for special education

- *Self-contained class:* children with disabilities have their own class
- *Service coordinator:* the person who works with child, parent, school officials, and social services

Working with social services

Throughout history, babies born with obvious disabilities have not fared well. They either didn't survive or were immediately institutionalized.

Today, with advances in medicine and education, a larger number of fragile children are raised in loving homes until they reach adulthood. Still, even parents who have the best of intentions can become emotionally, physically, and financially drained. When this happens, children may be placed in foster homes, government-funded group homes, or given up for adoption.

That's when government social service agencies get involved.

It's easy to criticize government agencies, and often social services agencies are represented in the media as callous or uncaring. In my experience, this is not usually true. I've yet to encounter a social services representative who's uncaring. These people are usually overworked, carrying caseloads that make success difficult. Social services offices are often underfunded and understaffed. And they're often bound by red tape that could make a bureaucrat scream. But most are not uncaring, and some specialists choose this field because they are Christians and feel called to work for social justice for these children.

We need to view them as potential allies, not enemies.

In most churches across the country, you'll find a growing number of foster families. You don't need to request a list from social services to find these folks. They have a strong word-of-mouth communication system, and they know fellow caregivers who might be struggling. Pray for ways to connect with foster families who are on the frontlines of caring for children with special needs, and watch how God will work.

Consider what happened with my friend Susan. While searching for a job, she came across an ad in the paper advertising for a "child advocate" in the court system. It was a volunteer position requiring four weeks of training in order to learn how to visit children in foster homes and then act as a spokesperson during court proceedings.

With three busy children of her own and a need for a paying position, signing on for a volunteer role didn't seem like a solid career or economic move. Yet God seemed to be speaking to Susan's heart. After a few weeks of prayer, she went for an interview and began training.

It was during this time Susan's church decided to start a special needs ministry that would reach out to the community. No one could have predicted how Susan's new job and this new ministry would dovetail so beautifully. No one but God, that is. Many of the children she served had behavioral and learning disabilities. Her free training and firsthand contact with needy children provided much needed help at church.

Another church planned a holiday party to serve foster families in their community. Children at the church made invitations and decorations, purchased gifts, and baked refreshments for the party. They led games and were intentional about welcoming and including children with special needs from the foster families that came to the party. Then the church kids prayed for the visitors and the needs of the foster families.

Who is God using to interact with special needs children and their families through the courts in your town? Tell them what you're doing. God may bring about a partnership.

Working with group homes

Like most parents, Lynn and Larry Tremel expected their daughter to grow up, move away from home, and have a family of her own.

More than 25 years ago they knew that would probably never happen. At 5 months of age, Megan failed to thrive; by age 3 she was diagnosed with multiple physical and intellectual disorders, including epilepsy and cerebral palsy. As her body grew into womanhood, her social skills remained at a preschool level.

"Megan walks and talks," said Lynn. "She's very social, but not highly teachable. She's not interested in learning how to dress herself, brush her teeth, shave under her arms, or take a bath." Naturally, Lynn and Larry are concerned for Megan's future. Emotionally, they've not yet been able to visit a group home for Megan.

"There's a school in Wichita, Kansas, that teaches life skills to young people like Megan. I'm praying about sending her there before we consider a private group home nearby."

The Tremels are like many parents facing retirement years with an adult son or daughter with special needs. Although Megan has older sisters who'll look after her, their parents don't expect them to take her into their homes.

The Tremels are like many parents facing their retirement years with an adult son or daughter with special needs.

"We've taken legal action to become Megan's adult guardians, and set up a living will for her care," said Lynn. "We don't want to put Megan in a group living facility just because we're getting older. We want to do it because it's the best thing for Megan."

Many group homes are privately funded Christian facilities. These homes long for the support of local churches in their community. You can partner with them by holding worship services at the home or offering transportation to your church's services or special events. Your church can join in fundraising efforts and provide counseling for parents, siblings, and grandparents.

LuAnn Ruoss keeps in contact with group homes in Bakersfield, California, where she was the director of special needs ministry at the First Presbyterian Church. "I've learned that it takes time and patience to build relationships. Some people are defensive toward the church because they've been treated so badly," says LuAnn. "I've tried to be consistent and do all I can to show how much we care. Now, the directors call me when a resident needs assistance moving to a new place. I get a group from church, and we get the job done."

Identify the group homes in your community. Set up appointments to find out what they need and how open they are to your involvement. Let the group home suggest what a partnership might look like and, as LuAnn suggests, be willing to move slowly. Trust takes time.

Working with community events

If you want to reach people, it helps to go where they are.

For many families who have children with special needs, several events have become regular highlights. Having your ministry volunteers actively involved provides a great opportunity to build a relational bridge between your ministry and families in your community.

If you want to reach people, it helps to go where they are.

Have the Olympics come to your town lately?

Many churches encourage their members to get involved with local Special Olympics. This international organization is dedicated to empowering individuals with disabilities to become physically fit, productive, and respected members of society through sports training and competition. Special Olympics offers children and adults with special needs year-round training and competition in 32 Olympic-type sports.

In 2010, more than 3 million athletes challenged the world to play united in the hopes of one day living united. They shared their message of unity at events in more than 170 countries. Children and adults who participate improve physical fitness and motor skills, develop greater self-confidence, and enjoy a more positive self-image. They grow mentally, socially, and spiritually; and they enjoy the rewards of friendship.

The goals of the Special Olympics don't specifically include participants knowing, loving, and following Jesus, but time spent serving and meeting special needs families is time well spent. You'll help your volunteers build a greater heart for these with developmental disabilities and also forge relationships.

Help the children at your church learn about the Special Olympics through a free curriculum available for download at getintoit.specialolympics.org.

Host a basketball team.

If your church has a gym, you can partner with the National Wheelchair Basketball Association. With 200 teams nationwide, there are bound to be other teams to play and an opportunity for children in wheelchairs to still get some hoop action.

Plus, many of the typical basketball teams have a team chaplain. By providing that service for the team you host, you'll have weekly opportunities to invite children and their families to your church. For more information, check out nwba.org.

Help shape other events.

Your community probably has dozens of golf tournaments, fun runs, craft fairs, neighborhood theater presentations, holiday parades and picnics, art shows, and concerts. Find out who organizes them, and provide someone from your ministry to help the planners see those events through the eyes of someone with disabilities.

It's likely that adapting the event so it's accessible to children with special needs won't take much—except for intentional inclusion. A gentle and helpful approach is almost always met with interest in cooperating.

Become known as an advocate for children with special needs not just in your church, but also in your community. If your church has a passion for helping these families—and that passion extends beyond your church walls—you'll be perceived as truly interested.

Ask parents of children with disabilities for help connecting with grassroots associations in your area that offer parental support and resource networks. These are excellent places to distribute fliers and other information announcing your ministry.

One source for agency connections that may be open to you is through local colleges or universities. Check with the staff in the college of education. Professors who work with special education courses are often highly connected and know which agencies are serving your community. While you're on the phone, ask for an appointment. Use that time to share your vision for your church, and ask about potential partnerships with the college. Are there students looking for unpaid internships? Is there research that the professor wants to conduct that wouldn't interfere with your program—and might bring some resources and grant money flowing in to fund your efforts? How can you connect with agencies that might want to know about your program? Be open to connections that might develop as you stay in touch.

Don't be discouraged if any community agency is less than receptive at first. Especially if they've seen church special needs ministries come and go, they may be hesitant to depend on you for consistent involvement. It's important not to make promises you can't keep. If you can't reliably provide transportation to your church each Sunday, say so. It's better to follow through on a monthly commitment than fail to keep a weekly commitment.

Don't be discouraged if any community agency is less than receptive at first.

And if you need a vision for why partnerships can be worth pursuing, keep in mind these words from former President George W. Bush:

"When governments, business, and individuals work together to build a welcoming society, Americans of every ability will benefit" (June 19, 2001).

That's true, you know. There's tremendous benefit in not reinventing the wheel, not reproducing services that are already available. By working with or alongside existing agencies, other churches, and willing community groups, you can expand the scope of your ministry without having to build everything from scratch. And you can concentrate on doing what you do best—what you bring to the mix that's unique and valuable.

THE INCLUSIVE CHURCH BLOG

Amy Fenton Lee's blog represents social networking at its best. "The Inclusive Church Blog is helping today's leaders better include children with special needs," says Amy. "It features the best practices from churches of all sizes, including ideas for how to effectively teach a Bible lesson to a child with learning differences. Samples of special

Just for you

Reaching out into the community can put you in contact with people who don't share your values or goals. That's okay—that's part of being salt and light in the world. What counts is that you're there, giving of yourself. That you're there listening. That you're there ready to serve.

Thanks for initiating relationships that God can use in powerful ways. Pray daily for God to work in his time and in his way to bring opportunities for your ministry to connect with children with special needs and their families.

Dear God,

Thank you for the chance to be your ambassador in this world. What a privilege! Bless the efforts of our special needs ministry and protect our hearts.

In Jesus' name, amen.

needs ministry documents such as intake forms, behavior management guidelines, and a gluten-free-approved food list are also included on the blog. The Facebook feed for The Inclusive Church runs links to articles and documents from other websites that may be useful to special needs ministry leaders."

With its goal of "helping churches successfully include children with special needs," The Inclusive Church blog is worth putting on your favorites.

theinclusivechurch.com
Facebook.com/TheInclusiveChurch
Twitter: @SpecialNeedsKidmin

11

FACILITY AND LIABILITY CONSIDERATIONS

by Pat Verbal

"I was glad when they said to me,
" 'Let us go to the house of the Lord.' "
—PSALM 122:1

Perhaps you think of David when you read this familiar psalm, but it always reminds me of Katherine and Jim Harrison.

When the Harrisons and their daughter, Jenni, relocated to Plano, Texas, they were anxious about finding a church home. Jenni was deaf, and like many people who are hearing-impaired, she couldn't read sign language. They had to find a church where Jenni could worship and be involved in ministry programs.

Like Jenni, some people who are hearing-impaired have the ability to follow what you're saying in conversation by reading lips. But that's of little help in a church sanctuary where platform speakers are a distance from the audience.

In the past, Katherine and Jim had been so frustrated searching for a place to worship that they considered giving up on attending church. They found that few churches provided a sign language interpreter and those who did were considered community leaders in special needs ministry.

Today there are other options for assisting people with deafness or hearing loss. Thanks to computers and media screens, worship services can include closed captioning that works much like closed captioning on television or movie screens.

A typist, often a court reporter, enters every word that's spoken into a computer with special software. The text is viewed on a TV monitor that can be seen by the congregation.

Most of the churches the Harrisons visited didn't have a viable program for the deaf but expressed an interest in putting one in place—someday. But this family's problem was that Jenni needed it now—not someday.

That's when the Harrisons found Prince of Peace Lutheran Church in Carrollton, Texas.

"Jenni was the catalyst," said Rev. Stephen Wagner in a story reported in the *Dallas Morning News*. "We were presented with a need that was right in our face…We'd done some research. We knew that if we could put together a ministry for the hearing-impaired that we would meet a need in our community."

The technology—called a CART program—is expensive and has been slow to catch on, but it's a solution that works with any hearing-impaired person who's able to read. That includes not only people who are deaf, but also people who are older and have sustained hearing loss. Anyone who can follow along as text moves across an elevated screen can benefit.

The Harrisons were finally able to worship together, complete in the knowledge that their church valued them and cared about Jenni's walk with the Lord.

Creating friendly facilities

A computer software program, video screen, and fast typist probably weren't the first things you thought of when it came to turning your church sanctuary into a space that's friendly for a special needs ministry, but it could be that simple. At least for churches that are seeing the average age of their membership creep upward, a program like the one that helped the Harrisons may be a true blessing. It doesn't take a total hearing loss for some church members to be unable to understand what's said in a large auditorium.

For most children with disabilities, your current classrooms are already equipped to meet their needs. Adaptations for them may be required more in your teaching styles and lessons than in the classrooms themselves. Children—and adults—with physical disabilities will be most affected by the limits of your church's physical facility.

Bring it up at your next building committee meeting

All new commercial construction is required to meet standards set by the Americans with Disabilities Act (ADA), as are buildings that are used for community meetings. If your facility is used as a preschool or school or if community groups use it for meetings, your building must be ADA compliant.

If your church building is one of those beautiful, old, stately cathedrals, some remodeling may be required to meet the standards described in this chapter. Still, there are many items on this list you can accomplish—perhaps by taking advantage of skilled craftsmen who are already in your congregation.

Pull together a meeting with qualified church leaders and members of the facility team. Be clear that attending the meeting will in no way commit them to donating the materials or labor needed to make all the modifications on the list. Rather, you're asking for the help of these professionals (and caring amateurs) to determine what can be done, what it will cost, and how to get the most bang for your buck.

CLOSED-CAPTIONING INFORMATION

To read articles on closed captioning, see "How Shall They Hear" at captioningtheword.com/pdfs/JCR_2002_11.pdf

You need this information, but more importantly your team may catch the vision and choose to step up and do some of the work. If possible, invite several people who use walkers, wheelchairs, and canes to speak to the team. They're valuable consultants.

Once you know how much money you might need, brainstorm with the church finance committee about a partial or complete renovation. Consider what funds are available. What means can you use for raising funds from the community? What are the obstacles standing in your way?

Do what you can do

It's easy to look at an older facility and wonder how you could ever possibly turn steep stairs into a wheelchair-friendly entrance. You may be tempted to think, "Well, we'll just change the facility when we build a new building." So the remodels are put off for another year…or decade…or longer.

Don't focus on changing everything. Instead, do one small thing and let the momentum build from there. Even a handrail where one didn't exist before will draw attention—and give you an excuse to celebrate with a ribbon cutting. Let people see that even if it's a slow process, the church is taking steps forward to include people with disabilities.

AMERICANS WITH DISABILITIES ACT

Upon the recommendation of the National Council on Disability, President George H.W. Bush signed into law the Americans with Disabilities Act in 1990. For a copy of the ADA, visit the U.S. Department of Justice's website at ada.gov/pubs/ada.htm.

One of the churches I worked with took three years to add an elevator and crosswalk that connected two educational buildings. If you think that sounds like a long time, you've missed my point. It's this: The people advocating for children with special needs didn't give up. It took three years, but it happened.

Another church carried children's wheelchairs up and down the stairs every Sunday. Members of this church couldn't afford to renovate, but they said it cost nothing to have some men with smiling faces and sturdy backs on hand to welcome children with special needs.

Whatever adaptations your facility may need, God already knows about them. He looks at your church's heart, which is where accessibility truly begins. With God's help—and your nudging—people's hearts can be renovated and redecorated to welcome all children in Jesus' name.

Here is an excellent guide developed by Joni and Friends that will help you evaluate your church's facility (find it at joniandfriends.org/static/uploads/downloads/Church_Facility_Accessibility_Checklist.pdf). How are you doing at providing a space devoid of these barriers?

Church facility accessibility checklist

Basic Accessibility

❑ Yes ❑ No Is it possible to get from a parked car to any area in the building without going up or down a step or steps?

❑ Yes ❑ No Are 1 in 25 parking spaces handicap accessible?

❑ Yes ❑ No Is the slope of walks not greater than 5 percent?

❑ Yes ❑ No Are walks of a continuing common surface uninterrupted by steps?

❑ Yes ❑ No Do walks have a level platform, the top of which is 5 feet if the door swings out onto the platform or towards the walk, or 3 x 5 feet if the door doesn't swing onto the platform?

❑ Yes ❑ No Does the platform extend at least 1 foot beyond each side of the doorway?

❑ Yes ❑ No Is the fire alarm both light and sound cued?

❑ Yes ❑ No Are service animals permitted in church buildings?

Signage

- ❑ Yes ❑ No Are Braille signs posted where needed?
- ❑ Yes ❑ No Is there a slightly raised, brightly colored abrasive strip to warn of open staircases?
- ❑ Yes ❑ No Are the characters and numbers on signs sized according to the viewing distance from which they are read?
- ❑ Yes ❑ No Are raised letters and numbers on signs raised a minimum of 1/32 inch (0.8mm), in a simple font, and accompanied with Grade 2 Braille?
- ❑ Yes ❑ No Are signs matte, or another non-glare finish?
- ❑ Yes ❑ No Where permanent signs are used to identify rooms, are the signs installed on the wall adjacent to the latch side of the door or on the nearest adjacent wall?
- ❑ Yes ❑ No Is the middle of the sign 60 inches above the floor?
- ❑ Yes ❑ No Can a person approach the sign within 3 inches without running into an object or standing within the swing of a door?

Ramps

- ❑ Yes ❑ No Do ramps have a slope no greater than 1 foot rise in 12 feet and width of no less than 36 inches?
- ❑ Yes ❑ No Do ramps have handrails on both sides?
- ❑ Yes ❑ No Are handrails 32 inches above surface of ramp?
- ❑ Yes ❑ No Are handrail surfaces smooth?
- ❑ Yes ❑ No Do handrails extend 1 foot beyond the top and bottom of the ramp?

Entrances and Exits

- ❑ Yes ❑ No Is at least one primary entrance to each building usable by individuals in wheelchairs? (It is preferable that all or most entrances and exits be accessible to, and usable by, individuals in wheelchairs or persons who are otherwise disabled.)

Doors, Doorways and Hallways

- ❑ Yes ❑ No Do doors have a clear opening of 36 inches or more? Are they operable by a single effort? (Note: double doors are not satisfactory unless they operate by a single effort or unless one of the two doors meets the 36-inch width requirement.)

❑ Yes ❑ No Are there any automatic doors?

❑ Yes ❑ No Are hallways at least 36 inches wide?

Floors

❑ Yes ❑ No Is the floor on the inside and outside of each doorway level for a distance of 5 feet from the door in the direction the door swings?

❑ Yes ❑ No Are sharp inclines and abrupt changes in level avoided at door sills?

❑ Yes ❑ No Are floors on each story at common level or connected by a ramp?

Worship Center

❑ Yes ❑ No Can people participate fully in worship?

❑ Yes ❑ No Can people hear? Is there adequate amplification of sound; e.g., is there an induction loop system or miniature broadcasting system which can be adapted to existing sound systems?

❑ Yes ❑ No Are there interpreters for those people who are deaf or hard of hearing?

❑ Yes ❑ No Can people see? Is there adequate lighting to enable participation in worship? (Light sources should be located so there are no shadows on speakers or interpreters.)

❑ Yes ❑ No Are large print Bibles, hymnals and bulletins available?

❑ Yes ❑ No Is space provided for wheelchairs? Does a person in a wheelchair have seating options?

❑ Yes ❑ No Do at least two or more seating spaces have extra legroom for persons with crutches, walkers, braces, or casts?

❑ Yes ❑ No Can people take communion without climbing steps?

Restrooms

❑ Yes ❑ No Is there at least one accessible restroom located on each floor?

❑ Yes ❑ No Do entrance vestibules, doors, and vision screens allow sufficient clearance for wheelchair passage?

❑ Yes ❑ No Do stalls have a turning space of 5 x 5 feet to allow traffic of individuals in wheelchairs?

❑ Yes ❑ No Is there at least one stall that is at least 36 inches wide (42 inches preferred)?

❑ Yes ❑ No Is there a 48-inch clear depth from the door to front of commode to allow a wheelchair in the stall?

❑ Yes ❑ No Is the door at least 36 inches wide and does it swing out?

❑ Yes ❑ No Are there grab bars on each side, which meet specifications, fastened securely to the wall at the ends and center?

❑ Yes ❑ No Is the toilet seat 17-19 inches from the floor?

Water Fountains

❑ Yes ❑ No Is there at least one water fountain on each floor which is usable and accessible by a person affected by a disability?

❑ Yes ❑ No If coolers are wall-mounted, are they hand-operated, with basins 30-36 inches from the floor?

Telephones

❑ Yes ❑ No Is there easy access to a telephone?

Elevators

❑ Yes ❑ No If your facility is multi-story, does it have an elevator?

❑ Yes ❑ No Is Braille used on the control panels in the elevator?

❑ Yes ❑ No Is the cab at least 68 x 51 inches?

❑ Yes ❑ No Does the door have a clear opening at least 36 inches wide?

Transportation

❑ Yes ❑ No Does the church provide transportation for people who are unable to drive?

❑ Yes ❑ No Does the church own a wheelchair accessible van?

How to comply with Americans With Disabilities Act (ADA)

Not everyone reading this book will be in America, so please forgive the constant references to American law. If your church is elsewhere, by all means work to comply with your own standards.

But the process described below will probably be useful whether you're in Canada, England, or India. Adapt it as necessary.

1. Plan ahead.

The time to take federal, regional, and city codes into consideration is at the front-end of any new building project or building renovation. A mistake or oversight made on a planning sheet or blueprint is easy to correct. Once construction is under way or finished, modifications are remarkably expensive.

Determine to meet every standard. Hold yourself accountable, not only because the building inspector will, but because barriers you fail to remove in your facility will work to keep people who need to be a part of your fellowship out.

2. Do your homework.

Obtain copies of the ADA requirements, and give them to your architect and building contractor. These construction professionals are already familiar with the requirements, but you want to be certain. You want to be sure that you and the construction professionals are on the same page when one of you says, "Let's make sure we meet the requirements." If you're working from the same document, there won't be surprises halfway through the project.

Be up to date on emerging technologies that might impact how you deliver services to children with special needs. You may need to have more electrical outlets and more circuits in rooms that might have medical monitoring equipment that travels with some children. It's less expensive to make electrical and plumbing accommodations proactively rather than after the fact.

3. Be clear about your priorities.

Most church building programs are an exercise in compromise.

The worship team would like a full soundboard that's the envy of any recording studio; it eventually settles for six microphones and a mixer. The counseling ministry wants a suite of offices that presents a professional image; it eventually is happy with better soundproofing and a reception desk.

It's easy to get lost in the process unless it's absolutely clear that no matter what other compromises are made, compliance with ADA regulations is non-negotiable. Ask architects to provide written confirmation that building plans and construction drawings comply with all ADA requirements.

And be sure that your legal counsel includes contractual terms in design and building contracts that require your architect and building contractor to fix and pay the costs of any construction that does not meet ADA standards. Once the facility is constructed, reconfirm that the facility meets all ADA requirements during a separate walk-through just for this purpose.

4. Be your own watchdog.

During construction or remodeling, keep an eye open for common mistakes. Local officials usually review construction planning documents to make sure that state and local building and fire-code requirements are met, but they often aren't authorized to enforce federal laws like the ADA. Consequently, if they sign off on blueprints and you okay them as well—assuming that ADA concerns have been monitored—you might well be assuming responsibility for any ADA oversights yourself.

This is not to imply that construction professionals deliberately try to cut ADA-mandated accommodations from building projects. But even a simple construction project can be a labyrinth of details, and unless someone is specifically looking out for ADA interests, it's easy to make mistakes. Anyone who's survived a home kitchen remodeling project knows how complex even a small project can become; imagine putting together a church building!

5. Show up and wander around.

Here's your chance to wear a hard hat! You've been a watchdog, but nothing beats showing up and checking in now and then. Most ADA mistakes occur in the building design, but many occur during the construction process. ADA mistakes that occur during construction can often be avoided if an architect or an ADA consultant visits the construction site and monitors progress to make sure the building is being constructed according to plan. Don't be afraid of paying a few dollars to hire a professional to do this once or twice.

6. Follow through, follow through, follow through.

Inspect completed work carefully. Identify mistakes and take action to have them fixed. And do it not just because it's the right thing to do.

The Department of Justice is responsible for enforcing the ADA on newly constructed public buildings. Private individuals may file complaints about inaccessible facilities with the department, or they may file their own lawsuits in federal court alleging ADA violations at facilities. Don't find out the hard way if ADA applies to you in your new facility—be diligent, and ensure complete ADA compliance so you won't upset any prospective visitors who have disabilities.

Liability considerations

As children's leaders, we take the health and safety of all children very seriously. Provisions for children with special needs are probably covered under your church's general liability insurance, but it's good to check with your church's insurance provider and legal counsel. You might want to take care of this before meeting with a church leadership team to recommend creating a special needs ministry; it's a question that might come up.

Some programs ask parents to complete liability release and care forms that clearly state children will be cared for by non-medically certified volunteers. Using this sort of form ensures the parents know exactly what level of care you can—and can't—provide. It's clear and helps manage expectations.

Do not imply that you have trained medical professionals available if it's not true. The fact that you have a licensed therapist or pediatrician in the congregation who's probably in the building on Sunday morning does not constitute attending staff. Parents of children with special needs want to know what to expect from you as you care for their children. Let them know completely and accurately; they'll appreciate your candor.

If you use release forms, present them in as loving a manner as possible. Be sensitive; some parents have been turned away by Christian educators when disclosing information about their children. Your goal isn't to scare parents away, but rather to communicate your desire to prevent emergencies and give the safest, highest-quality care possible.

While forms are important, one-on-one conversations are even more so. Talk with parents about their children. Give parents the opportunity to share their hearts as well as medical information. These parents know how to fill out forms; they've completed hundreds of them. But your focus is on more than a child's diagnosis. Use the check-in and background time to communicate your love for each child to the parents and to minister to parents themselves.

Please also know that no permission or authorization form makes you immune to lawsuits. If your staff and volunteers are negligent in the care of any child with or without disabilities, charges can be filed against your church. Negligence is negligence—there's no excuse for it, whether or not a permission slip was signed.

Your goal is to gather information, provide better care, and enhance relationships that God can use to build bridges. Having paperwork signed is important, but it's not an end in itself.

Your form should include...

- ❑ Usual contact information: child's name, age, address, e-mail address, and date
- ❑ How to reach parents at home, work, in the church building, and on their cell phones
- ❑ Space for the parent to identify the specific disability diagnosis or diagnoses
- ❑ Child's level of communication skills: speech, reading, writing, or sign language
- ❑ Brief history of child's response to separation and play with others, plus anything the parent(s) feel is important for you to know
- ❑ Name and phone number of child's primary physician
- ❑ Known allergies—to foods, drugs, and insects, for example
- ❑ Information concerning assistance the child might require—with food, hygienic needs, and sleep, for example
- ❑ Information regarding common behaviors—fears the child experiences or seizures, for example

In the interest of being comprehensive, you might also include the following authorization/release language. This is especially important if you'll be caring for children in a respite-care setting, where parents aren't in your facility as you care for their children.

Be mindful that you'll want your insurance provider and/or legal counsel to review any forms you create.

Sample authorization/release language

I have fully disclosed to ____________________ [name of your church] all pertinent facts about my child(ren)'s special needs, and I accept full responsibility for failure to do so. I understand the volunteers and staff want to provide the best possible care for my child, and I've done all I can to help them meet that goal.

If my child is enrolled in the respite program, I authorize the staff to provide any required special treatments or procedures to my child while in respite care. I will provide written authorization, instructions, and all necessary supplies and equipment for these procedures.

In case of an emergency or accident, I understand that the _______________ [name of city] Emergency Medical Services (911) will be called. I authorize EMS to administer any medical treatment, medication, or appliance deemed necessary by the EMS. I also authorize transportation by EMS to the nearest appropriate medical facility, as determined by EMS. I understand that I will be responsible for payment of all EMS, hospital, and physician charges for emergency services to my child.

I have read the above permission/authorization statement and agree to the terms designed in each.

Signed:____
(Parent/Guardian)

Date: ____

Just for you

Initiating or expanding your special needs ministry is risky. All the funds you need may not appear. All the volunteers you need may not sign up. Most of the families and children you want to serve might greet your grand efforts with a mighty yawn. After all your work, maybe just one child will respond.

That's success!

One child is worth it all. One soul. One family touched with Jesus' love expressed through a caring church.

Pray for those you hope will respond to your special needs ministry. It is okay to ask God to send enough families and children that you get slightly overwhelmed because that keeps you dependent on him.

But remember: One child is worth it all. One child is enough.

Dear God,

Thank you for the chance to serve children with special needs and their families. We praise you for the opportunity to communicate your love through word, touch, and smiles. Thank you for already knowing the names of every child who this ministry will touch. We can't wait to meet them and serve them as you've served us.

In Jesus' name, amen.

12

SERMON OUTLINES TO GET YOU STARTED

by Jim Pierson

A Letter From Dr. Pierson

Dear Pastor,

Since the late 1960s, I've spoken for many churches and conferences, encouraging listeners to open their hearts and church programs to people with disabilities and their families. In doing so, I've used several sermons. The following four are my favorites.

"Uniforms of Love" encourages Christians to show that they care about people with disabilities by following some practical suggestions. After preaching the sermon, I've frequently heard, "I can do those things. Thank you for making it so easy."

"At His Feet" reviews how Jesus responded to people with disabilities in his ministry. It also outlines what churches typically do and explores what churches and individuals in the audience could do.

"The Accessible Great Commission" drives home the point that everyone, regardless of ability, needs easy access to God's love

through Jesus. The term accessibility *is a well-known disability concept. The basic interpretation of accessibility is physical—how to negotiate a building with ease. However, in the Christian world, it also means spiritual accessibility.*

"Faith, Friendship, and Disability" is my personal favorite. Referring to the well-known story of how four friends brought their friend with a physical disability to Jesus for healing, this sermon stresses the importance of friendship in helping people with disabilities get to and actively join in the life of a congregation.

Because of my years of experience working with many wonderful human beings with disabilities, I've incorporated their stories as illustrations in these sermons. I'd urge you to substitute your own illustrations from the lives of people you know, so your sermons ring true and you speak with passion.

The statistics presented in these sermons were accurate at the time of this writing but may have changed. You can do a quick double-check via the Internet.

I share these outlines hoping they'll serve you well as you lead your congregation in embracing ministry to—and with—those who have disabilities. As these sermons and your own Bible study will confirm, there's a rock-solid biblical foundation for special needs ministry.

So please—adapt these messages as you will. Add to them. Delete what's not appropriate for your church at this time. Use them any way you can to present this truth: God loves people with disabilities. He welcomes them into his kingdom. We can do no less than to welcome those same people into our churches.

Sincerely,

Dr. Jim Pierson
President Emeritus, CCFH Ministries
www.ccfh.org
Knoxville, Tennessee

Uniforms of Love

SCRIPTURE READING: *JOHN 13:34-35*

Introduction

God's plan for getting his love to people is simple: He sent Jesus to demonstrate his love. Before returning to his Father, Jesus left instructions: "And then he told them, 'Go into all the world and preach the Good News to everyone' " (Mark 16:15). And then there's this: "Your love for one another will prove to the world that you are my disciples" (John 13:35).

God's plan is us. We wear the uniform of God's love. Just as emergency professionals wear instantly recognizable uniforms, the Christian's uniform of love should be equally as obvious. The 54.4 million people with disabilities in America need to be able to approach a loving Christian and expect a positive response.[1] Let's talk about how we can communicate love to people with disabilities.

1. Respond to the person, not the disability.

- React to the person with cerebral palsy, not the cerebral palsy. David's brothers saw a spoiled younger brother. God, because he looks at a person's heart, saw a king of Israel.
- Instead of reacting to the hand movements and communication quirks of a person with autism, a uniform wearer will see the potential of sharing the enriching love of Jesus.

2. Look at the person.

- When we make eye contact with someone, we acknowledge that person's presence. Do keep in mind that staring is one thing—giving a friendly look is another.
- Whether you're in a shopping mall, grocery store, or at church when you encounter a person with a disability, notice. A friendly smile from someone wearing the uniform of love encourages acceptance and lifts the spirits.

3. Touch the person with a disability.

- Touching suggests friendship. Jesus touched people who were blind, deaf, mentally ill, and who had leprosy.
- A touch from someone wearing the uniform of love can cut through the isolation some people with disabilities experience.

4. Do ordinary activities with the person who has a disability.

- Get to know the person's world—school, family, and daily schedule.
- Send a birthday card or other special-day card. Communicate that you're aware of the other person's world—and it counts to you.
- Share your life with the person who has a disability. Be open and real.

5. Encourage the person's family.

- Families are forever changed by disabilities. Disability is a major stress on marriage.
- Respite is a major need.
- There are four times of predictable crisis for families experiencing disability: when the diagnosis is given, when the child starts school, when school is over, and when parents realize they cannot provide care. Be there for families at these critical times!
- In Mark 9:17-27 Jesus showed sensitivity when he asked a young father (whose son the disciples couldn't heal), "How long has this been happening?" Jesus encouraged the father simply by engaging and recognizing the child's existence.

6. Share Jesus.

- People with disabilities are just people. They have souls, which need to be nurtured by God's redeeming love.
- People with intellectual disabilities and other developmental problems can be taught the message of God's love.
- Encourage your church to start a disability and special needs outreach. In doing so, you'll be welcomed as someone who wears the uniform of love.

Conclusion

God's love is important to all of us, regardless of ability. People with disabilities need to know about Jesus. As a wearer of the uniform of love, share the message of God's wonderful Son, Jesus, with people—including people with disabilities. Doing so makes an eternal difference.

At His Feet

SCRIPTURE READING: *MATTHEW 15:30-31 (NIV)*

Introduction

As a believer in the Lord Jesus Christ, I'm required to love people. And as long as those people look like me, think like me, talk like me, and cheer for the same football team, loving is easy. But when the people are different, the "love everybody" directive is harder to manage.

Today I want to talk about loving people whom I'm required to love—even if they're different from me. People with disabilities need the love of God's people, too.

People with special needs were a major part of Jesus' ministry. Recognizing his concern, they flocked to Jesus.

In today's Scripture passage, we learn that people with every kind of disability were brought to Jesus and "laid...at his feet." That makes sense when we note earlier that "he went up on a mountainside and sat down."

Let's explore how Jesus responded to these people with disabilities, how society responds, how the church responds, and what we as individuals can do when people with disabilities come into our lives.

1. How did Jesus respond when people with disabilities were "laid...at his feet"?

- He dealt directly with them.
- He involved the person in the plan. Jesus asked a man with a physical disability if he wanted to be healed (John 5:6) and a man who was blind what he wanted Jesus to do for him (Mark 10:51).
- He touched people with leprosy (Matthew 8:3).
- He thought helping people was better than following arbitrary rules. The Pharisees were furious when Jesus healed a man with a shriveled hand on the Sabbath (Mark 3:1-6).
- He was sensitive to the families experiencing disability. He asked a young father how long his son had been disabled (Mark 9:20-24).

2. How does society respond when people with disabilities are "laid at its feet"?

- American society, primarily through the legal system, has opened up to people with disabilities.
- Since 1975, a mandatory education act has required every school system to provide a free and appropriate education for every child regardless of his or her abilities.

SEEING THE REFLECTION OF GOD

R.C. Sproul, an author and the founder of Ligonier Ministries, has spent a great part of his life teaching on God's sovereignty. But it was his granddaughter, Shannon, born with a severe disability, who gave him a personal perspective on timeless doctrine.

"God is 100 percent sovereign even over these tragic things. How else could he make the promise to us that all things work together for good for those who love God and are called according to his purpose?" says Sproul. "My hope and

- In 1990 the Americans with Disabilities Act made society more accessible by making it easier for a person with disability to ride a bus, use all public facilities, and become employed in their community.
- The Special Olympics demonstrates what people with disabilities can achieve.
- The media portrays people with disabilities as valuable.
- It would have been great had the church led the way with these initiatives, rather than the legal community.

3. How does the church respond when people with disabilities are "laid at its feet"?

- The situation is changing—for the better.
- An increasing number of churches are making their Sunday school programs inclusive by having a trained assistant accompany a child with a disability to Sunday school, children's church, and other programs.
- Churches offer families who have children with disabilities respite care.
- More seminars, training materials, and information in general are available to assist churches in starting disability ministries.
- The church is doing a better job of serving people with disabilities.

my confidence is in a God who is sovereign and who cares and who is determined to bring good out of evil and to work all these things together for good."

Sproul has seen his son and daughter-in-law demonstrate the sacrificial love of Jesus time and again, as they count their daughter as one of their greatest blessings.

"People look at my granddaughter, and all they see is the tragedy. And that's why people even get angry and say, 'This child should have been aborted!' They don't see the image of God in Shannon. But my son sees it and my daughter-in-law sees it."

The Sprouls remind us that all children are a blessing from God, not just the healthy ones.[2]

4. How do you respond when people with disabilities are "laid at your feet"?

- We're not suggesting that a person can necessarily be healed of a disability, but we can provide "healing" with a positive attitude toward the person.
- We can look at the person rather than turning our heads.
- We can greet the person rather than walking by or altering our path.
- We have an awesome responsibility. We become our Lord. We are his hands, eyes, and feet. We need to treat people with disabilities as Jesus treated them.

Conclusion

Can we do any less than follow Jesus' example when it comes to responding to people with disabilities? The fact is that each of us—regardless of ability or physical traits—is made by our wonderful Creator, and each of us is invited into a meaningful relationship with Jesus.

The Accessible Great Commission

SCRIPTURE READING: *MATTHEW 28:19-20*

Introduction

People with disabilities were often recipients of Jesus' three-year earthly ministry. Matthew, Mark, Luke, and John report Jesus' interactions with people who were disabled with leprosy, blindness, mental illness, speech problems, deafness, and physical impairments. Jesus' Great Commission included them as well, and the church must reflect his concern. In our congregation, is the Great Commission accessible to everyone—even someone with a special needs diagnosis?

1. Regardless of ability, everyone has a soul.

- A person with a disability is first and foremost a person.
- The most valuable part of a person is the soul, and the soul needs to be redeemed and nurtured.
- The Great Commission is clear: Everybody everywhere is invited to hear and respond to the gospel.

2. Regardless of ability, the soul needs salvation.

- The disabilities that cause the most concern in teaching the plan of salvation are intellectual disabilities and developmental delays.
- Persons who are blind can learn Braille, persons who are deaf can read sign language, and people with other disabilities can learn the gospel if it's presented in a way that will overcome their learning difficulties.
- Are persons with disabilities, especially those with intellectual disabilities, still accountable for their sins? Yes, if their mental age permits it. Can people with intellectual disabilities understand how to become Christians? Yes, if they're taught.
- They have other spiritual needs as well: fellowship, accountability, learning God's Word, worship, prayer, giving, and service.

3. Regardless of ability, persons with cognitive deficiencies can be taught the gospel.

- People can establish relationships, lessons can be geared to the proper level, and appropriate language can be used. With a lot of prayer and perhaps over a long period of time, the gospel can be lived and taught.
- Why would we consider those conditions too high a price to pay to cooperate with the Great Commission?

4. Regardless of ability, everyone has the need to use their special gifts in service for the Lord.

- God has a purpose for all of his children.
- The "weaker member" factor is important (1 Corinthians 12:22).
- Everyone's unique gift helps the kingdom function.

5. Regardless of ability, everyone should be given the opportunity to be a part of the body of Christ, fellowship with God's people, and have the hope of heaven.

- Meeting together with people who share our faith is a part of being a member of God's family. Sharing meals, time, joys, troubles, lessons from the Bible, and our love for our Lord improves our abilities no matter how disabled we are.
- Knowing that someday we will be at peace with our Lord in heaven brings hope to every day of our lives.

Conclusion

The Great Commission is all-inclusive. The church and its programs must be accessible to everyone. People with disabilities must be welcome and as actively sought as everyone else to make our message of inclusion ring true.

Jesus' command in Luke 14 is specific. He tells us we are to go out into the streets and bring in the poor, crippled, blind, and lame. This is not simply a ministry of benevolence, because we gain much from their inclusion. William Hendriksen in his New Testament Commentary on the book of Luke reminds us, "What minister cannot bear testimony to the fact that some of the finest lessons he ever learned were given to him by the poor, the small, the sick, the handicapped, the dying?"[3]

Faith, Friendship, and Disability

SCRIPTURE READING: *LUKE 5:17-26*

Introduction

Friendship is a beautiful word in the Christian community. Having friends that share our faith is a source of encouragement. Furthermore, most of us are part of a church because a friend invited us.

In the world of disability, the friendship connection is often missing. The story of the four friends who brought their friend to Jesus for healing speaks to the church today (Mark 2:3). Our friendship with people with disabilities can make an eternal difference in their lives. Let's look at four ways of providing friendships that emerge from the story.

1. People with disabilities are valuable.

- It would be interesting to know how the five became friends. Did they grow up together? Was the man's disability a birth defect or the result of an accident? Whatever the cause of the disability, the four saw their friend as valuable and important.
- People with disabilities want affection, acceptance, and accomplishment. Our positive attitude toward them can help.
- Seeing people with disabilities as valuable and worthy of our respect and time will help the friendship connection.

2. Get involved in their lives.

- Nothing happened until one of the four friends got a stretcher and said, "Let's do something."
- The focus of our involvement is their spiritual development. A growing number of churches are opening their hearts and programs to people with disabilities and their families. Children with autism are given buddies to help them adjust in a Sunday school class. Couples can leave their children with special needs at the church building with qualified caregivers while they enjoy a rare time of respite.

- Disability ministry in a local congregation is a positive way to get involved.

3. Receive from the person with the disability.

- If we complimented these four men for their act of kindness, they might tell us how much their friend did for them.
- Real ministry is reciprocal. As we minister to people with disabilities, they minister to us.
- In special needs ministry, it is ministry *with*—not ministry *to*—families affected by disabilities.
- When our friends with disabilities embrace faith in Jesus, they become our brothers and sisters. They have God-given gifts that can enrich our lives.

4. Provide hope by sharing Jesus.

- The four friends knew the source of true rehabilitation—having the soul touched by Jesus' love.
- Getting our friends with disabilities to Jesus should be our focus. After they know Christ, they should participate in the life of the church.
- Isaiah's prediction will be realized: "And when he comes, he will open the eyes of the blind and unplug the ears of the deaf. The lame will leap like a deer, and those who cannot speak will sing for joy!" (Isaiah 35:5-6a).

Conclusion

Find a person in your neighborhood or a family who has a child with special needs and invite them to join you at church. Your actions will say, "You are valuable." Get involved with them. Acknowledge their spiritual gifts. Tell them about Jesus. Your friendship will make an eternal difference.

ENDNOTES

1 census.gov/newsroom/releases/archives/income_wealth/cb08-185.html

2 "When Disability Hits Home," Joni and Friends Television, www.joniandfriendstv.org

3 William Hendriksen, New Testament Commentary: Exposition of the Gospel According to Luke. (Grand Rapids, MI: Baker House, 1978), p. 725.

13

SPECIAL NEEDS HEROES

Reproducible Bulletin Inserts

by Larry Shallenberger

These 10 bulletin inserts about special needs heroes are for you. You may copy as many as you like, as often as you like, and use them any way you like.

They're designed to be two-sided bulletin inserts or fliers and distributed as people enter church. Our hope is that over the course of 10 weeks, the members of your church who read these personal accounts will recognize that people with special needs have made—and are making—a significant contribution to the church. They're certainly not people you'd want to turn away at the door.

Though—sadly—that's what happens sometimes. It may be because of our attitude toward people with special needs or simply because someone in a wheelchair can't reach or open the door.

Along the way your church members will be challenged to consider how they'd feel if they were to become disabled or if they were disabled and attending your church. This is a low-key, low-pressure way to raise the awareness of readers to the need for special needs ministries in your congregation.

Billy Graham

Billy Graham may always remain the world's favorite evangelist. Dr. Graham has appeared on the Gallup organization's list of "most admired men" 55 times. Read that again—55. That's a lot of admiration!

Billy Graham may also long be remembered as one of the world's most famous sufferers of Parkinson's disease. Parkinson's disease is a debilitating ailment that impairs its sufferers in several ways.

People with Parkinson's disease experience chronic stiffness in their muscles. Some patients complain of chronic arm pain and others experience tremors in their arms, jaws, necks, or faces. Some Parkinson's victims report a loss of balance and dizziness and have difficulty walking.

Billy Graham soldiered through many of these symptoms as well as other health problems brought on by advancing age, continuing to travel and speak in front of huge crowds that often filled entire stadiums. His calling to preach the gospel, expressed through the newly formed Youth for Christ International in the 1940s, continued for more than 50 years.

Graham was one of the first evangelists able to penetrate the Iron Curtain, openly preaching the gospel in public settings. He's preached in person to more than 80 million people and received both the Presidential Medal of Freedom and the Congressional Gold Medal.

Graham has proclaimed the gospel through 23 books, Decision magazine (1.4 million circulation), and his Hour of Decision radio show. He has further strengthened the church by founding Christianity Today magazine.

Though Graham felt the toll of Parkinson's disease, he continued to hold crusades and attract hundreds of thousands of listeners.

William Martin, author of *A Prophet with Honor: The Billy Graham Story*, quotes Graham as saying, "My mind tells me I ought to get out there and go, but I just can't do it. But I'll preach until there is no breath left in my body. I was called by God, and until God tells me to retire, I cannot. Whatever strength I have, whatever time God lets me have, is going to be dedicated to doing the work of an evangelist, as long as I live."

For Further Exploration

- Visit one of the shut-ins of your church—listen and enjoy a conversation about the history of your church. How could your church benefit from hearing these stories of how God has moved in your congregation? How can you help share these stories in ways you will be heard?
- What types of frustrations do you think Billy Graham experienced as he attempted to continue his ministry in spite of Parkinson's disease?
- How can your church help elderly people with special needs to enjoy their experience at your church?

A Passage to Ponder

"Not that I have already obtained all this, or have already been made perfect, but I press on to take hold of that for which Christ Jesus took hold of me. Brothers, I do not consider myself yet to have taken hold of it. But one thing I do: Forgetting what is behind and straining toward what is ahead, I press on toward the goal to win the prize for which God has called me heavenward in Christ Jesus."

—Philippians 3:12-14 (NIV)

Prayer

Dear God,

Sometimes our bodies and our energy betray us. We fall short of what we want to do for you. We pray for health so we can serve you and tell all those we come in contact with about the joy of knowing you. At times, we're tempted to quit. Help us press on for the prize that is you.

In Jesus' name, amen.

Don Bartlette

Dr. Don Bartlette has experienced enough abuse, neglect, and physical ailments for bitterness to take hold in his life.

Instead, he's made a career of speaking a message of love and tolerance. Bartlette has presented his workshop "Macaroni at Midnight" more than 7,000 times at foster care training sessions, churches, and public schools. Dr. Bartlette has been featured on the Focus on the Family radio program, and Messenger Films is producing a movie based on his life.

Bartlette was born with a severe cleft palate into a poor Chippewa family who lived in the hills of North Dakota. Ashamed of his son's disfigured face, Bartlette's father never called the boy "son." A rugged, athletic man who drank excessively, Bartlette's father beat him violently.

Bartlette was 9 before he started attending school. He arrived speaking in grunts and sign language and was daily ridiculed by other children. His peers hit him and spit on him. One teacher forced Bartlette to stay in the janitor's closet rather than the classroom as a way of avoiding disruptions that came with having Bartlette in class. Bartlette moved through the school system in spite of his academic shortcomings because teachers didn't want him in their classrooms for another year.

At 12, Bartlette was still unable to speak. He became a loner, clothing and feeding himself from the town dump. He committed minor crimes, was arrested, and then sent home on bail—where his father beat him mercilessly.

Bartlette's life turned around when a new woman moved into town. The first day they met, she taught him how to wash a car. Later Bartlette trusted her enough to let her teach him how to use silverware. She then patiently taught him to read, write, and talk.

Asking his benefactor why she was helping him when no one else would, the woman showed Bartlette a Bible.

She arranged for Bartlette to receive plastic surgery. After seven years of tutoring, he graduated as valedictorian of his high school class. He continued with higher education and became a social worker, counselor, and educator.

For Further Exploration

- What personal risks did the woman in Don Bartlette's story assume when she befriended him?
- Imagine that a boy with a cleft palate like Bartlette lived next door to your church. What are some of the risks involved in attempting to reach out to this child? What would some of the benefits be?
- Think through your circle of influence. Who are the people in your life to whom it would be a risk to extend compassion? Commit to praying for these people this week. Ask God if he'd like you to share his love with one of the people on your list.
- Consider watching the film *Patch Adams* (rated PG-13) with a group of people from your church. After the movie, discuss how the risk of getting involved with people affected the life of the main character. Discuss the reason why individuals and churches sometimes pull back from the adventure of touching lives.

A Passage to Ponder

"But a Samaritan, as he traveled, came where the man was; and when he saw him, he took pity on him. He went to him and bandaged his wounds, pouring on oil and wine. Then he put the man on his own donkey, took him to an inn and took care of him."

—Luke 10:33-34 (NIV)

Prayer

Dear God,

Like the travelers in the parable, we're on a journey. As we go, give us courage to see and meet the needs of other travelers on the way. We apologize for times when we have passed people by. Forgive us for ignoring the needs of people for whom you have died. Teach us to be neighbors to the hurting.

In Jesus' name, amen.

Dave Dravecky

Dave Dravecky's career has evolved from player (baseball) to survivor (cancer) to player (baseball) to survivor (cancer) to counselor (life).

Dravecky began his major league baseball career as a starting pitcher for the San Diego Padres. During his fifth year with the Padres, he helped his team reach the World Series. In 1987, Dravecky went to the San Francisco Giants in a blockbuster seven-player swap. Undeterred at being cast off by his former team, Dravecky threw a no-hitter the opening day of the 1988 season.

In October of the same season, doctors detected cancer in Dravecky's pitching arm. Surgeons removed half the muscle in his pitching shoulder, but Dravecky refused to accept that his baseball days were behind him. He began an intense program of rehabilitation, and a year later Dravecky pitched a 4-3 victory over Cincinnati, earning the cheering admiration of both fans and peers. He wrote about his journey in the stirring book *Comeback*.

The cheering evaporated when Dravecky's humerus bone snapped while delivering a pitch in a game against the Montreal Expos. Extensive radiation treatments had weakened the bone, and his dramatic comeback was officially over. Cancer made an unwelcome return the following year. The doctors had no choice but to amputate his arm. There would be no second comeback: not for a pitcher with his pitching arm gone.

Today Dravecky is a popular speaker and author. He contributed to the Encouragement Bible and has established the national cancer ministry Outreach of Hope. Through his former magazine, The Encourager, and his website, endurance.org, Dravecky provides practical, biblical counsel for cancer and amputation survivors. Several Christian ministries such as Focus on the Family and Promise Keepers have featured Dravecky's story.

Dravecky's baseball comeback may have lasted only for a season. However, his emotional and spiritual comebacks from cancer have forged him into a source of hope for thousands of people who are literally battling for their lives.

For Further Exploration

- Think of a time in your life that was particularly difficult over an extended period. Whom did you turn to for support? How would the situation have turned out had those supportive people not been around—or had refused to help?
- When a family member has a special need, the entire family experiences stress. Take a mental inventory of the programs that your church offers. How can your church provide support for a family stressed by special needs?
- What are some ways your church can provide emotional and practical supports for people who don't have families to rely on? What new programs might help?

A Passage to Ponder

"But God has combined the members of the body and has given greater honor to the parts that lacked it, so that there should be no division in the body, but that its parts should have equal concern for each other. If one part suffers, every part suffers with it; if one part is honored, every part rejoices with it."

—1 Corinthians 12:24b-26 (NIV)

Prayer

Dear God,

Thank you for connecting us as you've knit us all into one body. Help us stop seeing ourselves only as individuals, but as part of the church. The joys that affect one of us affect all of us. The pain of one is everyone's pain. In this bigger sense, we lift "our" pain to you. Heal us. Help us work together to support and encourage the weak.

In Jesus' name, amen.

Dennis Byrd

On November 28, 1992, Dennis Byrd was a specimen of physical prowess. Byrd was a 6-foot-5-inch, 270-pound defensive end for the New York Jets.

On November 29, 1992, Byrd couldn't unclasp his own chinstrap. During a home game against the Kansas City Chiefs, he spun around the offensive line and collided with another teammate while attempting to sack the quarterback. Within seconds of hitting the hard turf, Byrd knew he was paralyzed.

One moment Byrd was an NFL gladiator; the next he was unable to move. As he lay in a hospital bed, Byrd didn't know if he'd ever be able to hold his wife, Angela, or his daughter, Ashtin, again.

As the ambulance rushed him to the hospital, Byrd summoned his faith in God. In his autobiography, *Rise and Walk*, he writes, "It was at that moment, en route to the hospital, that I turned everything over to the Lord, that I put it all in his hands...I had no idea what lay ahead of me, but I knew that this was going to be a test."

Byrd was a quadriplegic. The football field collision had shattered the fifth cervical vertebra in his spine. The doctors couldn't promise Byrd he'd ever walk again.

Although he lay limply in bed, Byrd's mind and spirit were active. On a poster board that he could see, the hospital chaplain wrote the words, "For I reckon that the sufferings of this present time are not worthy to be compared with the glory which shall be revealed in us" (Romans 8:18, King James Version).

Byrd spent months in the hospital undergoing experimental therapies and surgeries. All the while his childhood faith was being refined through his fear, discouragement, and intense frustration along the way. Two months after his accident, Byrd was able to take small steps.

Byrd's miraculous rehabilitation captured the nation's attention. The week before the Super Bowl, Bob Costas interviewed Byrd and his wife before a live national audience. Byrd had the opportunity to share how his faith in Jesus was a source of strength during his long months of rehabilitation. Less than a year later, Byrd walked to the middle of Meadowlands Stadium to the cheers of 75,000 fans.

For Further Exploration

- Dennis Byrd drew from his history with God to get him through dark months of rehabilitation. Schedule a few quiet hours, and journal your history with God. Write down the milestones that you and God have encountered together. How can remembering these times be a source of strength for you in the future?
- Byrd relied on encouragement from his wife, friends, and the hospital chaplain to find the strength to commit to rehab. Why is encouragement so important in overcoming obstacles?
- How can your church be a place of encouragement to those dealing with special needs?

A Passage to Ponder

"Praise be to the God and Father of our Lord Jesus Christ, the Father of compassion and the God of all comfort, who comforts us in all our troubles, so that we can comfort those in any trouble with the comfort we ourselves have received from God."

—2 Corinthians 1:3-4 (NIV)

Prayer

Dear God,

When we're afflicted with suffering, our first response is usually to grumble. Help us to respond to you in faith, trusting that you will comfort us. It's only after we've felt your comfort that we're able to comfort the afflicted around us. We trust your plans, even when we cannot understand them.

In Jesus' name, amen.

Frank Peretti

Frank Peretti is famous for penning best-selling novels concerning spiritual warfare. However, long before he wrote about unseen battles, he had battles of his own.

Peretti was born with a life-threatening condition known as cystic hygroma. Cystic hygroma is a birth defect usually found on the neck. A mass growing on a sufferer's neck threatens to close the airway, and the mass often causes the bone structure of the skull and teeth to develop incorrectly.

When Peretti was born, the doctors misdiagnosed the small lump on his neck. The doctors assumed that the forceps used during a harrowing, middle-of-the-night-blizzard delivery had caused the lump. Peretti's nervous parents were told that the lump would dissolve within a few weeks. Two months later, doctors performed emergency surgery to remove a baseball-sized lump from Peretti's throat.

At first, the surgery seemed to be successful. Then young Peretti's tongue began to swell out of his mouth. During his neck surgery, the doctors removed some of Peretti's lymph nodes. Consequently, the remaining lymph nodes were forced to secrete an infection into his tongue. A fluid oozed from Peretti's mouth that turned black when it encountered the air.

The enlarged tongue made speech development a torturous task. Seven tongue surgeries carved his tongue into a stub creating a whole new set of problems for Peretti. His speech was slurred, and by the time he went to kindergarten, his tongue again drooped from his mouth. The drooping tongue, drooling, and black fluid turned Peretti into a target for teasing. And because the cystic hygroma also delayed Frank's physical development, he was unusually small. Only his mother's loving but firm authority kept him in school.

Peretti's family and church were a haven from the daily abuse he suffered at school. Children in Frank's Sunday school class welcomed him as a friend and prayed for his recovery.

Peretti's books for adults, including *This Present Darkness* and *Piercing the Darkness,* have sold in excess of 9 million copies, and children have enjoyed his popular *Cooper Kids Adventure Series.* He's impacting the world through print, speaking engagements, and video production.

For Further Exploration

- Peretti praises his church family for being a safe place for him as a child. What were the potential challenges Peretti's church faced by welcoming his family into their congregation?
- How is your church a safe place for people with special needs?
- How can the children of your church help make your church a safe haven for children with special needs?

A Passage to Ponder

"A man with leprosy came and knelt before him and said, 'Lord, if you are willing, you can make me clean.' Jesus reached out his hand and touched the man."

—Matthew 8:2-3a (NIV)

Prayer

Dear God,

We're all disfigured in some way. Some of us wear our disfigurements visibly. Some of us wear our scars on the walls of our souls. Please teach us to be gentle with each other. Remind us that our words can be like stones; forgive us for the times we've thrown unkind words at people who are different from us. Use our kind words to build safe havens for the hurting.

In Jesus' name, amen.

Ginny Owens

Ginny Owens discovered the piano at the young age of 2—at about the same time that she completely lost her sight. Her difficulty seeing was so evident at birth that her parents and doctors easily noticed her poor vision. Surgeries were attempted, but none saved her sight.

Owens' parents were determined their daughter would have the same experiences that other children enjoyed growing up. In an online interview at TodaysChristianMusic.com, Owens recalls "climbing tall trees, riding bikes, roller skating, digging in the backyard, determined to make it to China." And music was a large part of her experience.

In spite of her parents' drive that their daughter be no different from any other child, potential employers certainly viewed her as "different." Too different to be hired.

Owens graduated from Belmont University, cum laude, with a degree in music education—and a requirement to successfully complete student teaching. But when she applied for teaching jobs, principals refused to hire her. Owens believes her blindness prevented her from being hired.

Then a publisher took an interest in Owens' music. She signed as a writer, then produced a three-song demo album and signed with Michael W. Smith's Rocketown Records in 1999. The same year, she performed at the prestigious Lilith Fair, a concert honoring female artists, in Nashville, Tennessee. Her first album, *Without Condition*, introduced her to the Christian music scene and won her the 2000 Dove Award for New Artist of the Year. "Blessed," a song she co-wrote with Cindy Morgan, earned her a 2001 Dove Award for Inspirational Song of the Year.

Several network television shows such as *Felicity, Charmed, Roswell,* and *Get Real* have featured Owens' music.

While Owens resists being classified by her disability, she acknowledges that she has had to make adjustments in the way she connects with her audience. A typical singer uses facial cues to determine how the audience is responding. Owens listens to the audience, guessing whether they're listening.

For Further Exploration

- Close your eyes. Think through what it would take you to accomplish the simple routine of getting dressed in the morning if you were sightless. What systems would you have to put in place for you to be able to wash your clothes, find them in the morning, and dress yourself?
- What would it take for you to be able to attend and participate in church?
- Think through your worship service and Christian education experience. How do these opportunities appeal to senses other than sight? If you were unable to see, would you be able to participate fully?

A Passage to Ponder

"Open my eyes that I may see wonderful things in your law."

—Psalm 119:18 (NIV)

Prayer

Dear God,

We're all blind in some way. We've been blinded by sin, by pride, by greed. We don't see the world accurately. Sometimes we don't see other people at all. Open our spiritual eyes so we become aware of your presence in our lives. Help us see the needs of people around us. Forgive us for choosing to be blind to them.

In Jesus' name, amen.

Heather Whitestone McCallum

When Heather Whitestone was only 18 months old, she contracted the Haemophilus influenzae virus. To combat the dangerously high fever, doctors gave her two powerful antibiotics.

It's uncertain if it was the fever or the medicine, but Whitestone's hearing was reduced to 5 percent in one ear—and zero percent in the other ear. Doctors told Whitestone's parents their little girl would never speak, drive, or advance beyond a third-grade learning level.

With the help of her parents, Heather Whitestone shattered the limitations her doctors placed on her. At the age of 6, she began taking ballet lessons. Her mother taught her to use her limited hearing and to read lips. Following high school she wanted to join a Christian dance company, but submitted to her mother's desire that she attend college. She attended Jackson State University, which didn't have a dance program, so she continued to dance on her own.

Learning dance routines was particularly difficult since she couldn't hear the music's rhythm. She learned to count the music in her head and memorize her dance routines in 30-second blocks. Through unflagging perseverance, she mastered a single dance routine in a year's time.

When she decided to enter the Miss America competition, she prepared herself by attending the pageant the year before she planned to enter. She realized that she would be distracted by the crowd noise, and it would interfere with her ability to hear the beginning of her music. Undaunted, she performed in countless nursing homes and churches to train herself to focus while dancing. Her first competition interviews failed because she couldn't understand what the judges were saying. However, Whitestone tried again and won entrance into the pageant.

In front of 40 million television viewers, Whitestone used her hard-earned dancing skills to witness to her faith...and she won the title.

In 2002, Whitestone married. She continues to use her position of influence as a former Miss America to spread the gospel with her books *Believing the Promise, Listening With My Heart, Let God Surprise You,* and *Heavenly Crowns.*

For Further Exploration

- When someone who can't hear accomplishes something remarkable—such as becoming Miss America—why does it amaze people? What do you think our culture assumes about people who can't hear? can't see? can't speak?
- Imagine attending your worship services as a deaf person. How much of the experience would you be able to appreciate? What elements would you miss?
- How could your church make participating in worship services easier for those who can't hear?

A Passage to Ponder

"For this very reason, make every effort to add to your faith goodness; and to goodness, knowledge; and to knowledge, self-control; and to self-control, perseverance; and to perseverance, godliness..."

—2 Peter 1:5-6 (NIV)

Prayer

Dear God,

We thank you for Heather Whitestone McCallum's example of faith and determination. Forgive us for letting lesser obstacles keep us from accomplishing what you want us to do. Help us learn from our brothers and sisters who daily face the challenges of dealing with deafness, blindness, and other special needs.

In Jesus' name, amen.

Joni Eareckson Tada

At 15 years of age, Joni Eareckson placed her faith in Jesus at a Young Life camp. Three short years later, her fledgling faith was put to the test when she broke her neck in a diving accident. She became a quadriplegic and lost complete use of her hands. Eareckson committed herself to two long years of rehabilitation in order to learn how to hold a paintbrush with her teeth. Among her many talents, she's now an accomplished artist and illustrator.

Eareckson published her autobiography, *Joni*, in 1976. The book shares how Eareckson's faith enabled her to wrestle with the reality that, short of a miracle, she'd remain a quadriplegic the rest of her life.

World Wide Pictures released the movie *Joni* in 1979 and translated it into 15 languages. Joni and Friends ministry was founded at the same time and has influenced the lives of thousands of people with disabilities.

Eareckson married high school history teacher Ken Tada in 1982. Ken retired from teaching in 2004 and joined the ministry of Joni and Friends.

According to the Joni and Friends website, the Wheels for the World program has collected over 52,000 used wheelchairs, arranged for their refurbishing, and shipped them overseas. Medical staff fit these wheelchairs to both children and adults.

The National Religious Broadcasters honored her radio program "Joni and Friends" with the "Radio Program of the Year" award. The foundation has created retreat centers for families affected by disability. A sports camp provides specialized training for wheelchair athletes.

Eareckson Tada is a prolific author. Her nearly 50 books have included devotionals, art collections, and children's books. *Tell Me the Promises* and *Tell Me the Truth* both won awards from the Christian publishing industry.

Prior to her diving accident, Eareckson Tada never could have imagined the tremendous impact that her life would have on thousands of people. Small wonder one of her favorite Bible verses is 2 Corinthians 12:9b, " 'My grace is sufficient for you, for my power is made perfect in weakness.' Therefore I will boast all the more gladly about my weaknesses, so that Christ's power may rest on me."

For Further Exploration

- Take a look at the Joni and Friends Church Facility Accessibility Checklist located at joniandfriends.org/static/uploads/downloads/Church_Facility_Accessibility_Checklist.pdf. What did you learn about your church, and how inviting is it to those in wheelchairs?
- Borrow several wheelchairs from a health-care provider, and take a field trip of your church. How did you feel as you attempted to navigate your church by wheelchair?
- Eareckson Tada uses her story as a tool to tell others about Christ's work in her life. What is your story? How can you use that story to let others know about Christ?

A Passage to Ponder

"That is why, for Christ's sake, I delight in weaknesses, in insults, in hardships, in persecutions, in difficulties. For when I am weak, then I am strong."

—2 Corinthians 12:10 (NIV)

Prayer

Dear God,

We're weak people...but we hate to admit it. We like to imagine that we have power and influence. But without your power, we're lost, Lord. We invite you to work through our weakness so your power can work through us. We commit to you this power to care for the weak and to uphold the downcast among us.

In Jesus' name, amen.

Phil Keaggy

For Phil Keaggy, less is more. As a guitarist, he does more with 9 fingers than most guitarists can accomplish with 10.

Musician magazine ranked Keaggy in its list of the "100 Greatest Guitar Players of the Twentieth Century." His 1990 release *Find Me in These Fields* garnered both a Grammy nomination and the Gospel Music Association's Instrumental Album of the Year. His albums *Acoustic Sketches, 220, Premium Jams, The Wind and the Wheat, Beyond Nature, Invention, Majesty & Wonder,* and *The Lights of Madrid* have all scored numerous nominations and Dove Awards, the Christian music industry's equivalent of a Grammy.

With 9 fingers—not 10.

Keaggy's discography has stretched through 40 years. He's produced some 50 instrumental and vocal albums during his illustrious career. Classically inspired pieces, jazz, 16-bar rock riffs—he's a top talent no matter what direction the music takes him. And through projects such as *True Believer*, he sings the truths of the gospel with the unmistakable clarity of a tent-preacher.

With 9 fingers—not 10.

And that's one of the most amazing things about Keaggy's career: how seldom anyone mentions that he's missing 10 percent of a guitarist's most essential tools.

Like thousands of other children, as a youngster Keaggy expressed an interest in music. His father bought him a $19 guitar. And there's no evidence that his parents tried to steer him away from playing guitar in order to protect him from failure or disappointment.

Instead, Keaggy's parents allowed their son to pursue his passion with excellence. For Keaggy, excellence was an expression of his spirituality. In an interview in Fingerplay Guitar Magazine, Keaggy said, "I also want to encourage other guitar players to pursue a life of excellence, a life that has spiritual significance."

For Further Exploration

- Phil Keaggy's family was willing to nurture his interest in the guitar, although he had a physical disability. What are some ways that your church can nurture everyone's God-shaped dream—including the dreams of the physically disabled?
- Why do you think most people tend to focus on obstacles instead of opportunities?
- Schedule a time to tour through your church facilities with a group of friends and leaders. Consider inviting a person who uses a wheelchair to join your group. Do your facilities present any obstacles for physically disabled people in your church? What steps can your church take to make your building more welcoming to people who have physical disabilities?

A Passage to Ponder

"Love never fails. But where there are prophecies, they will cease; where there are tongues, they will be stilled; where there is knowledge, it will pass away."

—1 Corinthians 13:8 (NIV)

Prayer

Dear God,

You say all things are possible. Please forgive us for focusing on the obstacles instead of the possibilities. Forgive us for viewing people with special needs in terms of problems that need solving. Lord, we know that you have filled every one of us with immense potential and possibilities. We submit ourselves to you and to your power to work inside of us.

In Jesus' name, amen.

Rick Warren

Adrenaline. Talk with any preaching pastor in America, and you'll hear that the body's natural ability to create adrenaline is a vital part of preaching. Without adrenaline's energizing effects to sustain a pastor's stamina, most sermons would fall flat. In fact, psychologist Archibald Hart suggests that many pastors are addicted to the euphoric feeling that adrenaline brings.

Not so for Pastor Rick Warren. When adrenaline rushes through his veins, he feels ill. He was born with a brain disorder that prevents his body from assimilating the chemical. When a stressor triggers the release of the chemical in Warren's body, he feels symptoms such as fainting, headaches, dizziness, temporary blindness, and confusion. These conditions would make it hard for any pastor to fulfill pulpit duties, but Warren is in an especially challenging situation: At Saddleback Church in Southern California, he preaches to crowds totaling more than 20,000 people every weekend.

In an interview on his website, pastors.com, Warren writes about why it's painful for him to preach: "The very thing I need to speak to 5,000 people at one time is the very thing that harms my body...I think it's part of God's design that the guy who [God] chose to speak at Saddleback is also a guy who is really quite weak."

Treatment is an ongoing issue for Warren. When he was growing up, doctors treated him with epilepsy medication because they didn't know what else to do. The Mayo Clinic is currently involved with Warren's ongoing treatment.

During its first 15 years, Saddleback Church grew from 250 people to 10,000 people—and all without a permanent building. Warren and his teams scrambled to find 79 different locations to host their church. Talk about adrenaline!

Warren continues to preach, speak, and write—he's the author of several bestsellers—all while enduring his allergy to adrenaline.

For Further Exploration

- Download a sample stress test at stressdiagnosis.com and take the self-inventory. What would your life be like if you suffered an allergy to adrenaline?
- People are more aware of food allergies lately—such as allergies to gluten and peanuts. Ask those in charge of your church's kitchen, as well as your children's ministry director, what safety policies are in place to ensure the food your church serves is safe for everyone. If you use wheat-based bread for communion, what happens to someone who's allergic to gluten in the wheat?
- Unseen disorders, like Rick Warren's allergy, could be mistaken for a character flaw such as a lack of motivation. How should the church go about calling people to excellence without being insensitive to people who may have unseen impairments?

A Passage to Ponder

"But God chose the foolish things of the world to shame the wise; God chose the weak things of the world to shame the strong...so that no one may boast before him."

—1 Corinthians 1:27, 29 (NIV)

Prayer

Dear God,

In our pride we refuse to believe that we are weak. We like to forget that we still struggle with sin. We like to pretend that we can get through life on our own power. We are foolish. Help us to be "poor in spirit." Thank you for loving us, even through the weakness of our pride.

In Jesus' name, amen.

EPILOGUE

I WISH I HAD DONE MORE

by Kenneth Lay

It was my privilege to know intimately four special needs children during my ministry as a pastor, and their influence continues to impact my spiritual journey.

I learned early that such children have a mission, and as their stories unfold they continually touch lives in a unique way. As I reflect on their mission, I also look back on my own ministry to them and their families. This is my conclusion: I wish I had done more.

Mark was born with serious birth defects, and periodically he had to be hospitalized more than 100 miles away. His father was a public schoolteacher, and in an effort to be of help, I substituted for him on some of those occasions. At other times, I took Mark and his mother to the hospital. I wish I had done more. I wish I had ministered to the depth of the pain and the challenge to the faith of Mark's mother and father.

Jay was born with Down syndrome. When he was very young, I would hold him in my arms as we told the congregation goodbye after the morning worship service. He enjoyed that and so did I. But I wish I had done more. I wish I had put my arms around his daddy. I wish I had hugged his mom. I wish I had been more sensitive to the needs of his sister and brother.

Paul was born with a multitude of problems, including Down syndrome. He lived in another town, and we only saw him on special occasions such as at his brother's wedding when Paul, as the ring bearer, rode his Little Tikes bike down the aisle. I wish I had been more involved in his life through intercessory prayer, letters of encouragement, and more frequent phone calls.

Abby was born with cystic fibrosis and lived for 13 years. When she died, I held her mother in my arms and cried with her. Her mother is my daughter. I wish I had done the same for the mothers and fathers of all the others. I wish I had shed the tears I felt instead of holding them back in order "to be strong for the family." After all, Jesus wept with his friends at the grave of Lazarus. I have learned that hugs and tears sometimes carry more healing and strength than words of advice.

Special needs children can play a far greater role in our lives and the lives of our churches if we allow them to. Every church and every pastor should be personally involved in disability ministries. It allows the love of God to flow in all directions and produces a bond of heavenly fellowship. It calls for more than empathy; it calls for a sharing of emotions. Children (and their families) with special needs sometimes are ignored and not always loved. The blessing is ours when we love them, accept them, cry with them, and allow them to fulfill their mission.

I wish I had done more.

Kenneth Lay, a retired minister, now teaches Sunday school at First Baptist Church in Edmond, Oklahoma.